Stolen Beauty

D0111768

Stolen Beauty

HEALING THE SCARS OF CHILD ABUSE

One Woman's Journey

Amy Madden

SYREN BOOK COMPANY
MINNEAPOLIS

Published by
Syren Book Company
5120 Cedar Lake Road
Minneapolis, MN 55416
763-398-0030
www.syrenbooks.com

Printed in the United States of America on acid-free paper

ISBN 978-0-929636-74-0

LCCN 2006940504

Cover design by Kyle G. Hunter
Interior text design by Wendy Holdman

To order additional copies of this book, please go to
www.itascabooks.com

For my father, James Alfred Madden,

whose love, compassion, and generosity
still inspire me today.

Contents

Acknowledgments

I would like to thank everyone who encouraged me and believed in me during the birth of this book. It's been a long process, and my gratitude and love come from the deepest place in my heart.

My sisters, Micki, Angie, and Liz, who through the process of our lives have remained kindred spirits and have continually shared their love. To my brother, Mark, who was my angel in disguise.

My daughter, Megan, the little angel in my life, whose love, inner beauty, and unique ability to see things on a soul level at a very early age have been an inspiration to me since the day she was born.

My son Mark, whose kindness toward others has shown me that love and oneness really do exist.

My son Scott, whose humor and wisdom have never ceased to entertain and profoundly surprise me.

My mother, who taught me that survival is inherent.

My friend Carmen, my soul sister, whose extraordinary love and encouragement have kept me on track.

My friends Jake, Mel, Jim, Avid, Rhonda, and Matt,

whose encouragement throughout the process of writing this book has been very much appreciated.

My other editor, Barbara Ardinger, for her words of encouragement.

My Gurus Apolonia Fortino and John Armstrong at the Center for Inner Knowing in Atlanta, who moved me toward my true self.

My love, Gary, for showing me the depth in which love can be experienced.

Lastly, for every precious child in the world and especially those who have been abused. This book is for you. May you learn that your beauty belongs to you and no one can ever steal it away. You are the heart and the soul of the world. God bless each and every one of you.

Introduction

Dear Ed,

I am writing you this letter to let you know that I am sorry you had to spend the last nine years of your life in prison. However, I hope you were able to use your time wisely in reflection so that you understand that what you did to me, my sisters, and the other small children you abused was wrong. I hope you have received help, and if not, that you will seek it out now, through therapy (if it will help you) and hopefully through God.

You stole the innocence of my childhood and replaced it with something ugly and perverted. I don't know what your own childhood was like. I can only speculate. I knew your mother for a very brief time and experienced her venomous nature and mistreatment, so I can only imagine what living with her as an only child must have been like. I did not know your father well, as he was in his last dying days when he came to stay with us, but he seemed to be a kinder soul. However, you made a choice to continue the cycle of abuse. Possibly you blamed your mother or father, and because of that you were able to justify your own actions of abusing others. I can only believe that you were blinded by your anger and resentment and the pain of your own neglect or abuse.

Therefore, I can forgive you. I will pray that you have learned from your lesson in this life. I will pray that you are able to let go of the pain and anger inflicted upon you in childhood and move from harming others to healing yourself.

I will pray that you find peace within yourself so that you might come to love yourself instead of seeking out your distorted view of love and controlling it through abusing innocent children.

Most of all, I pray that you can find the strength to ask God to forgive you and that you can somehow forgive yourself.

Sincerely,

Amy

This is the letter I wrote to my stepfather, who made a choice, thirty-four years ago, to abuse me and my sisters when we were children. Taking advantage of Florida's twenty-year statute of limitations, my sisters and I filed charges as adults and saw him convicted. He was sentenced to nine years in the Florida State Penitentiary for his crimes against us.

My stepfather chose to abuse. He has paid a high price for those choices. We all make choices in this life, and it's those decisions that determine our paths, sometimes through pain and sometimes through love. It doesn't matter how well we have been able to convince ourselves that our actions are right if, in the end, they hurt other people; we will eventually feel the pain. This is the law of karma, and until we bring our choices to a conscious level and make love our goal, we will always have the burden of karmic debt. Karma is a concept from Eastern religions that comprises the entire cycle of cause and effect. It's the sum of all an individual has done and is currently doing. The effects of those deeds actively create present and future experiences, thus making one responsible for one's own life. The law of karma means that all living creatures are accountable for their karma and for their salvation, and it does *not* just mean we get that second chance in the next life, as many Westerners would like to believe. Many of us will experience that cause-and-effect cycle in *this* life, and, surprisingly, it can come around very quickly.

This book is a picture in words, told from an adult perspective, of the abuse I experienced. My purpose in writing is to explain how I was able to deal with the pain, shame, and anger of that experience. I use the word *experience* because it's important to understand that the experience of child abuse does not make us who we are. It is only that—an experience, a bad one, no doubt, but the experience itself doesn't make us a bad person. If I were to use the word *victim* to describe my experience, it might lead you to believe that I was blaming someone, so I hesitate to use the word because I believe there comes a time when we have to move from blame to forgiveness in order to get on with the process of healing and loving ourselves.

There also comes a point when each of us needs to recognize that life teaches us many lessons and that each person's lessons are unique. Every one of us has a path in life to achieve our very best. If we can learn to accept, to forgive, to live in the present by turning each bad experience into something beneficial rather than an adversity, then we will grow. The way I look at it, I had two choices. I could use my experience of abuse to bring positive awareness to others, or I could continue living in the past, dwelling on my pain, nurturing it to justify my own actions of inflicting pain on myself and others and validating my feelings of unworthiness. I spent some time on the latter path. I am now on the path of using my experience to promote positive growth.

I am sharing the unraveling of that process so that I can offer my insight to every child who has been abused.

Prologue

As children, we are innocent and unassuming. We are in constant awe and wonder at our surroundings, where even the smallest things become magical. I remember one hot summer day. How intrigued I was watching an ant carry a leaf twice its size with strength and determination that still fascinate me today. I also remember the delicate feel of a ladybug's dance circling my palm. I watched her tiny wings spread, preparing for flight, and then suddenly she changed her mind. I wondered if she liked me as much as I liked her. At night, looking up at the midnight sky and the twinkling stars, I believed they were holes in heaven where God could peek through and beam His light on the good people of the world. As a child I believed in God, but I also feared Him. I believed that only "good people" were privy to His light.

Some children never reach an age where they are able to experience nature's small wonders or contemplate a Higher Source. How tragic this is. No child should have to live a life of stolen innocence, a life of stolen beauty. No child should have to live with fear on a daily basis; no child should have to feel shame, humiliation, or guilt for something he or she had no control over. It is our duty as adults to protect our children. Not just our own children, but every child. We should ensure that all of their experiences are based on love. We need to help them learn self-respect and give them a sense of dignity and pride that will free them to experience all that life and nature have to offer. This is not a choice of *can* or *can't*. As adults, we have the power to provide a safe, stable, and loving future for our children. When we say we can't do that, we create lasting effects that will follow an abused child into adulthood.

Many adults who have survived abuse are able to cope in society at a normal level by burying the abuse deep within themselves. Others are able to cope by undergoing therapy, which might keep them functioning on a fairly normal level. Some individuals, however, are unable to cope, perhaps because the extent of the abuse was just too much to bear. Their abuse made them shut down, mentally or emotionally. Some children survive and grow up and continue the cycle by abusing their own children and sometimes even murdering them. They might even look outside the family and turn their anger toward others, which will eventually lead them to harm themselves. Whenever we inflict pain on someone else, it damages our own psyche, and when this happens, we must remember that these abusers were once children themselves, once innocent, creative, and lovable. That is who they were and who they would be today—if someone had rescued them.

We have to take back responsibility for *every* child. Ignoring a child's cry for help or blaming and ridiculing adults will not help them alter their behavior. Perhaps when they were children, we gave them back to the abuser. Perhaps we put the abused children in a foster home, where it's possible they received further abuse or neglect. When they grew up, perhaps we put them in jail without treating them or ignored them because we deemed them social misfits.

It is a fact that more than seventy-five percent of people who abuse were abused in some way when they were children. On any given day, you can turn on the news or read in the paper about the latest child abuse case. What is truly sad is that the stories we read and hear about are usually in the news because the child has been tortured, beaten, raped, neglected, or murdered by his or her parents or guardians. The child has spent his or her whole young life in an atmosphere of horror, but until the tragedy happens, no one knew what was happening. No one came to the child's rescue. As we read or hear about these tragedies, we look at each other and shake our heads. We ask ourselves, *how could anyone do such a thing to a child?* But as we look to abusers for answers, we don't like what they have to say. Usually they are pointing the finger at someone else or blaming a society that ignored them when their own childhood pleas for help went unanswered.

It's easier to blame abusers than to try to figure out a way to help them. We may ask questions, especially if we hear that the local Department of Family and Children Services already had reports filed on the child in question, but as soon as we turn off the TV or put the newspaper down, we forget about it.

With so many cases being addressed in the news today, it has become apparent that we clearly have a growing problem with our current system. While it is necessary to punish abusers, it is also necessary to try and rehabilitate them and break the cycle. Sex offenders constitute a large and increasing population of prison inmates, most are eventually released to the community without any kind of rehabilitation. The percentage of abusers who received help while incarcerated in 2004 was about ten percent. That means that once an abuser is free, he or she is very likely to continue down the same old path of abuse. The statistics for convicted physical abusers are difficult to find, because the Justice Department lumps physical child abuse into the violent crime category and does not disseminate the data.

After many years of blaming and punishing myself and asking myself why abuse had to happen to me, I finally found some answers. I began reading books and talking about my experience. It also helped me tremendously to open myself to the inner spirit within me, which is something all of us can do. It was through wonderful authors like Marianne Williamson, Neale Donald Walsch, Caroline Myss, and Iyanla Vanzant that I was able to find a sense of peace within myself. I was reminded that the heart is linked to the essence of who we are, which I believe is directly connected to God. These are my personal beliefs, and not everyone will agree with me, but for anyone who does believe there is a Higher Source at work in our lives, we must look to that source and not let fear or anger stop us. Many different names have been given to this Higher Source—God, Buddha, Allah, or Goddess. I choose God because that is the name I feel most comfortable with. Whatever we call the Higher Source, however, there is one common element that I believe binds us all together: *love.*

It's also important to become aware of what right and wrong feel like. Before we make a choice or take an action, we must ask ourselves several questions: *Will what I am about to do bring happiness or pain to myself or others? Am I being impeccable with my word? Have I handled an unpleasant situation with grace and compassion? Can I see without judgment? Can I listen with an open heart?* If we ask for help, the Higher Source at work in our lives can help us answer *yes* to all of these questions. All we have to do is ask.

Like me, many survivors of abuse have a difficult time believing there is anyone who can help them. We feel abandoned. We have lost our faith that there is a God who is there to help us. We have no sense of guidance. We have lost the ability to see who we are.

I say to abused children and adults, *It's never too late to start believing again. It's never too late to recover the faith you've lost. It's never too late to rediscover who you truly are.* The source of All That Is awaits each of us. He has never left us. He never will. He only wants what we want for ourselves—happiness.

If we can embrace the wonder of human life and live with the purpose of bringing happiness to others, we will be amazed at how quickly happiness returns to us. A good place to start is with our precious children. But this is a difficult task because, inside, we are all children struggling to gain our heart's desire, and in our struggles we adults sometimes overlook our sons' and daughters' desires. Sometimes we fail to recognize their most basic needs.

Child abuse doesn't have to end tragically. There are ways to overcome our past. This may be a dream to those who have grown into adulthood bearing the burden of their pain, shame, and neglect, but it's time to make their dreams a reality and help them realize that they are worthy of love and (more important) that they *are* loved. It's time for us to take our children back into protective arms and nurture their souls.

There are those who believe that "our destinies are mapped out long before we are born and it's up to us to find out, through love and giving, what that destiny is. Once we discover it, the universe will conspire to guide us."[1] I find this to be an interesting philosophy, and whether it's true or not, it may be easier for some to believe that it is through a loving heart we will accomplish our most precious gifts and our most favored desires. In the process we can raise our children to be healthy, happy, loving human beings.

This book recounts the process of my healing. I tell my story from the point of view of the child I was, as well as of the adult I am now as a result of my experience. I try to offer advice that I pray will give insight to my readers.

---

[1] Paulo Coelho, *The Alchemist* (San Francisco: HarperSanFrancisco, 1993), 40.

Stolen Beauty

CHAPTER I

Is There a God?

I was six when I began asking myself, *is there really a God out there?* It was 1966 and we were living in Anderson, Indiana, a small town about an hour outside Indianapolis. There was a feeling of desperation in my household that I recognized even at that early age. I had a brother, Mike, eight years old, and two sisters, Dianna and Lindsay, ages five and seven. Mom and Daddy had divorced the year before, and we were struggling to live on my mother's meager salary.

It was a difficult time. In the sixties, being a single mother with four children was not normal. Mom, twenty-five years old, was beautiful, but she was also a high school dropout with four children and no skills. She could not find a well-paying job and was forced to take a minimum wage position at an insurance agency. We moved from the bright, sunny home we had shared when my father still lived with us to a small, dark duplex. It was sparsely furnished. I remember a threadbare couch, perhaps one chair in the living room, and, in the kitchen, a small Formica table with chairs whose tattered plastic seats scraped the backs of my legs when I sat on them. The bedrooms were empty. All we had to sleep on were mattresses on the floor. Even now, all I remember is the feeling of emptiness I had while we lived in that space.

Daddy moved to Indianapolis, and we didn't see him for a year or two, during which time he did not pay child support. Mom, who (I've no doubt) was feeling hopeless and heavily burdened, remarried as soon as she could. I believe there was a feeling of desperation on her part that prompted her to marry so quickly. I am now convinced that her intuition was overshadowed by the need to care for her children. She had no idea the man she was about to marry, Ed Hayden, was drawn to her specifically because she had young children.

A few months after they were married, we moved again, this time to a house. It was old, but with its two stories it felt grand to us children. There were three rooms on the first floor and three bedrooms plus a bath on the second floor. The high ceilings made it seem even larger. I remember I was full of awe and excitement and felt that happier times were on the way.

But things deteriorated quickly. Soon after we moved in, so did Ed's parents. His father was dying of cancer and unable to manage the stairs, so a makeshift bed was set up in the dining room. Ed's mother, who was senile, moved into my brother's bedroom to live out her final days; Mike moved in with me and Dianna and Lindsay.

I don't remember Ed's father. He was only with us for a few weeks before he passed away, but his mother, who was with us for several months, left me with many unpleasant memories. I believe now that it was she who had had the biggest impact on Ed when he was a young boy. Even in her old age, when she could barely walk, she was an evil woman. My sisters and I believed she was a wicked witch. Every afternoon for as long as she was alive, Ed would make each of us go to her room, alone, after school and sit with her. Those dreadful moments still live in my mind. The curtains were always drawn, which made the olive green walls even darker and more sinister. She lay in the center of the room on a twin bed. I sat on a wooden chair next to her bed, but that was too far away for her. She always ordered me to sit on the bed where she could reach me.

Every day, she reached out with her gnarled hand and yanked my hair.

"This is heathen hair," she said. "Only sluts have long spaghetti hair like this. Next time you come in here, it had better be cut off or I'll do it myself. Do you hear me?" Her breath smelled of mothballs, and her eyes looked like they were going to pop out of her head. I was terrified of her.

Even though I doubted that she could carry out her threat to cut my hair, I always nodded dutifully and quickly so she would let go. I was always amazed at how strong her hands were. As soon as she released my hair, she grabbed my arm and pinched it. "Answer me, you little brat," she always said. "Did you hear me? Cut it off, or I will."

"Yes, ma'am," I whimpered, feeling like a trapped rabbit. As soon as her hold on me weakened, I bolted from the room in tears. Ed was always standing outside the door, eavesdropping. When I came out, rubbing my arm, he greeted me with a triumphant smirk.

I understand now that Ed's purpose was to put us through some of the torture he must have endured as a child, but at the time I was bewildered and frightened by his open display of pleasure at my pain and fear. If I had known what was to come after his mother's death, I would have prayed for God to keep her alive.

Her death in the early autumn marked the end of life for a woman who had lived more than eighty years and the beginning of a life that seemed, to a child, to last an eternity. It was my life. The abuse I endured lasted for six years. In those years I lost my childhood innocence.

Oddly, though, my first encounter with abuse happened before Ed began abusing me. I realize now that my path in life was set long ago and that those patterns would repeat themselves—that it was up to me to learn how to overcome them. I had just begun first grade, and, for reasons I can only speculate about, my teacher, Mrs. Beck, chose to take out her frustrations on me. The first time it happened was during lunch. I was standing in the front of the line with my best friend, waiting to walk to the cafeteria. My friend told me she had brought money to buy an ice cream after lunch and asked me if I had done the same. At that time, my mother barely had money to feed us, so we never got an extra dime for ice cream. When I told my friend I didn't have any money, she offered me one of her dimes and I thankfully took it. That's when Mrs. Beck turned on me. She grabbed my arm and jerked me out of the line. "Go to the end of the line, you little beggar," she hissed. "Beggars can't be leaders. You'll always be a follower."

The teacher's words stayed with me for a long time, and from that day forward I became the only one in class that she took great pleasure in humiliating. If my shoelaces were untied, she would make me stand in the corner. If I looked out the window to catch a glimpse of the winter snow or spring's first bloom, I was forced to lay my head on my desk for the duration of the class. I dreaded going to school. Many days, I went home and cried, but my mother thought my complaints were only a child's exaggeration. She was too caught up in her own life to take time out to confront my teacher.

Just as I didn't blame my mother then, I never blamed her later for my stepfather's abuse. To this day, she claims she had no knowledge of what was happening to me and my sisters, and although I have at times questioned her claim, I have finally come to believe that she really didn't know what was going on. To believe otherwise would mean that she was just as evil as Ed. I knew my mother was not evil. Dianna and Lindsay are more skeptical, however. They often ask, "How could she *not* have known?"

I believe that Mom was living in denial on many levels. After she and Ed were married, she gave birth to another child, my youngest sister, Susie. Now she had five children to raise, which tied her inextricably to Ed. Even though her intuition might have warned her that he had some serious issues, she was young and penniless. She may have rationalized that if there were no physical signs, then it wasn't happening. Sexual abuse was a taboo subject in the sixties. Even though it was happening, it was rarely reported. On another level, I suppose, Mom could have convinced herself it just couldn't be. Maybe she even asked herself, *what if it is true?* If she had found out it was true, she might have been forced to do something about it. With five children under the age of ten and no money, that was too daunting to even contemplate. I'm not making excuses for my mother. I just believe that at the time she was doing what she thought was best for us, and if the only way to do that was through denial, then that was her choice at the time.

As children we want someone to find out what's happening to us so that the pain and shame will end, but our fear stops us from telling anyone. Ed kept our fear alive with repeated threats. The worst threat was that he would kill my mother. The fear of living a life without her and having to live with him (or in some unknown place) became part of my psyche. It was this fear that brought my thoughts to God.

I remember thinking I had done something wrong and God was punishing me for it. We never went to church as a family, so I'm not exactly sure why I even believed there was a God who could be very good to some, but who also took pleasure in dealing out punishments to the wrongdoers of the world, including children. My guess is that I had heard other adults speak of Him this way and thought it must be so.

Then one day something happened—I thought it was a miracle—that validated my belief in God. My life was turning into something ugly and perverted. Shortly after the death of his mother, Ed began drinking heavily. The first stages of his abuse were verbal threats aimed at my mother and us, with the occasional belt beating if we misbehaved.

One Saturday, Mom had persuaded Ed to take us all to the drive-in. It was our first time, and we were all excited. Mom filled two large grocery sacks with popcorn and handed them to Mike and Dianna to add salt. They began fighting over who was going to go first. When Ed heard the squabbling, he pounded into the kitchen, his face puffy and red, his fists clenched. He ripped off his belt and slapped the side of the refrigerator. "That's it!" he roared. "None of you little shits are going. Now get your sorry asses upstairs and stay there!"

All four of us ran up the stairs, crying. Even Mike was crying as he stomped off to his room. A few minutes passed. Mike beckoned us all into his bedroom. He had a plan. Above his bed was a picture of Jesus that Ed's mother had left behind. We thought it was a picture of God. Mike suggested that we kneel down and pray to the image. It was our only chance of getting to the movies that night, but we weren't sure about the best way to pray. Finally we got down on our knees, two of us on each side of the bed, put our hands together, and looked up at the picture. Mike started out. "Please God, please let us go to the drive-in," he prayed. "We promise we won't fight anymore." We girls chimed in, repeating the prayer over and over with a fury of "pleases."

The image of us, children with no religious or spiritual guidance. praying with our whole hearts and souls to a God we knew nothing about, remains vivid in my mind today. We were still praying when Mom walked into the room a few minutes later and said, "Okay, kids, come on now ... you can go."

I was awestruck. A miracle had occurred! God had given us a quick response, and I was filled with such joy, and what I can only describe as love, that I started to cry. Mike looked at me like I was crazy.

"What are you cryin' for?" he asked. "Mom said we could go. It worked!"

Not sure why I was crying, except for the indescribable feeling of amazement, I wiped my tears. God had revealed Himself with a swiftness that made me turn back to the picture and look at Him with great reverence. He had answered our prayers. We were going to the drive-in. It was on that day and because of that insignificant event that I began to believe there might be an omnipotent power at work in our lives.

It's funny how little things can have such an enormous impact on a child. Perhaps, more than anything else, it was *hope* that struck me that day. If God would answer such a small prayer, then maybe there was hope that He would answer bigger prayers. At first my prayers were, "Please, God, make him stop being mean to my mom," and, "Please, God, make my stepfather stop doing these awful things to me." Later I prayed, "Please, God, just let me die."

But before the drive-in miracle, it had never occurred to me to pray for anything. I knew nothing about God and didn't know how prayer worked. As things progressed and my life turned to chaos, however, I began to feel unworthy to talk to God. I thought He was mad at me for something I had done so I prayed for Him not to be mad at me. At the same time I kept trying to figure out what it was I had done wrong. I knew He wouldn't answer me again until I had fixed it.

CHAPTER 2

The First Day

It was a beautiful Indiana September afternoon. The air was cool and crisp with the distinct smell a sunny autumn day brings. I was six and had entered first grade and life seemed perfect. As I stepped off the school bus, I noticed that the leaves were just beginning to don their fall wardrobe, and I picked up a maple leaf to smell it. Although it was a bit early in the season, my excitement mounted as I visualized myself jumping into a mound of freshly raked leaves. Then my thoughts quickly changed to the upcoming game of kickball across the street, and I ran into the house to change clothes.

I pounded up the stairs and into the bedroom, where I struggled out of my dress. The back door slammed, and I looked out the window to see which one of my siblings had beaten me out the door. It was Mike. I watched him tear across the lawn toward the garage. My attention next was drawn to a tiny movement below my window. Our cat, Samantha, had had a litter of kittens several weeks before, and Lucy, the runt of litter, who also happened to be blind, was sitting on the back porch step licking her tiny paw. I smiled briefly and tried to open the window to yell down at my brother to bring her back into the house. But the window was painted shut. Suddenly I caught a movement from the corner of my eye and turned to see my neighbor's dog, Meng, a really mean Chow, running toward our house. He was headed straight for Lucy. I began screaming and banging on the window with my fists, hoping to stop the dog or get my brother's attention. But it was too late. I watched in horror as Meng clamped down on the kitten's neck, shook his head viciously, then dropped her lifeless body from his jaws and ran off. I stood with my fists on the window, my head against the glass pane, and sobbed.

That was when Ed walked in.

"What the hell are you screaming and crying about?" He stood in the door, legs apart, trying to look bigger than his five-foot four-inch frame. His face was dark and distorted, his deep-set eyes glared at me, and his teeth, which were yellow and protruded slightly from his mouth, were clenched in rage. Waiting for my reply, he ran a hand through his slicked back hair. When I said nothing, he yelled at me again. "I asked you what the hell you're screaming and crying about."

The look on his face frightened me. I tried to explain about the kitten, but I couldn't get the words out through my sobs. He became disgusted and told me to shut up and stay in my room while he went downstairs to see for himself what was going on. As soon as he left, I started crying again. I knew I was in trouble, but I didn't know why. I was afraid of the unknown, I was afraid of his look, I was afraid of the way his jaw tightened when he spoke, the way his fists kept clenching and unclenching as I tried to speak. His body language told me that nothing would be okay when he returned, so I quickly finished changing my clothes.

When I heard the back door slam I ran to the window again. Ed picked Lucy up and dropped her, like a dirty sock, into a dustpan, which he handed to Mike. I felt sick and started to cry again, but I knew I had to get down there and help my brother bury her.

That was when I heard Ed's footsteps coming back up the steps. He stopped at the door again, a cigarette between his lips and his eyes like slits. He took a drag from his cigarette and smirked. "The cat's dead. But it was the best thing that could have happened to her. No one wants a puny, blind pussy anyway." He laughed at his own joke.

I was confused. I thought all animals mattered. Lucy was even more special because she was small and blind. My mouth began to quiver again as I looked at him.

"Jesus, don't you start your fucking crying again," he said. "Go into my bedroom. I'm going to show you something that will take your mind off that stupid cat."

I couldn't move. Was he going to beat me? He came forward and wrapped one hand around the back of my neck, something that would become customary. I cried out in fear and winced as he pushed me into his bedroom and ordered me to sit on the bed. He stood in front of me and began unbuckling his belt. I felt the hairs rise on the back of my neck, replacing the burning feeling his fingers had left. But instead of taking his belt off to hit me, as I was expecting, he dropped his pants and stood naked from the waist down in front of me. He began playing with himself.

"Do you know what this is?"

Terrified, I shook my head. I didn't want to look at him or at what he was doing to himself. I was confused and nauseated. I had never seen a man's body before. For it to be revealed in such a way had a sickening effect on me, because I knew it was wrong, horribly wrong.

"I'm going to teach you what this is and how it works and it's going to be our secret. Do you hear me?" he asked. "Now touch it."

I shook my head as hard as I could, biting into my lower lip until it bled. I didn't want to touch it. I was terrified of the bulging mass of flesh he was manipulating. I couldn't touch it. I started to cry again, but inside I was telling myself not to cry. Crying was what had gotten me into this mess to begin with. If I hadn't been such a crybaby over Lucy, maybe he wouldn't be doing this to me now.

"Touch it, goddammit!" he screamed. He grabbed my hand, placed it where his had been, put his huge hand over mine, and began moving my hand with his. I was crying openly when he finished his business.

He slowly pulled his pants up and buckled his belt. Then, reaching down, he grabbed my chin in a vicelike grip. "I'm going to be teaching you a lot of things," he said, "and if you ever tell anyone, I'm going to kill you and whoever you tell. Understand? That means if you tell your mother . . . I'm going to kill her. Got it? No one. And that includes your sisters. This is our secret, and you had better keep it, or you'll be sorry." Releasing my chin, he grabbed both shoulders hard and leaned over till he was eye-to-eye with me. "Do you understand me? You tell . . . they die."

I nodded shakily, unable to speak, and watched him leave the room.

I sat on the bed, shocked and numb. Never had I felt so lonely or isolated as I did in that moment. Never had I felt this kind of shame, a shame so big it seemed tangible. Never had I felt this kind of fear. His words, his menacing tone, the look on his face all made me aware for the first time that evil exists and it can strike at any moment. It was the first time I had ever felt any of these emotions, and it was devastating. My beautiful September day was now gray, almost black; the cloud of shame had descended. I wiped my tears. A few minutes later, I placed a lone yellow buttercup on the makeshift grave Mike had put Lucy in. Then the tears started again. I cried for her and I cried for myself.

CHAPTER 3

Reward and Punishment

I lost control of my life that first day and began living in a constant shadow made up of despair and loneliness. I had only brief glimpses of sunshine.

I find now that when I try to remember every day of those six years of abuse, I can't do it. I believe it's because so much of the abuse was the same thing, and I only remember the days when he would do something new and awful. I never knew why or how he would decide to do something different. I never knew why on certain days he chose me over one of my sisters. At the time, I thought I was the only one. That's what he wanted me to believe. As time went on, he became more and more confident, thus more demanding.

At first, he was entertained by forcing me to touch or fondle him. That lasted about a month. He would take off in the afternoons and come home while my mother was working, when he knew his chances of being caught were minimal. It was always after school, and he would often begin by coming into our bedroom to watch us change clothes. I always thought he was just looking at me, that he had singled me out and I was the only one. I could feel his eyes boring into my back, reminding me of the secret I was forced to keep because my life and my mother's life depended upon my silence. It wasn't until years later that it occurred to me he was picking out his prey for the afternoon.

His abuse continued to escalate. Soon he was touching and fondling me. He was invading my space, my body, my soul. My body would stiffen at the mere touch of his fingers. The pent-up anger and tears that I tried desperately to keep in check would leave me shaking with shame and disgust every time he touched me. But I knew that if I dared let my resentment show or give into tears of frustration, I would be punished and further humiliated.

He used reward and punishment to get what he wanted. My reward? If I let him do as he pleased, he would leave me alone for a couple of days. My punishment? A second day of abuse. The only reward was thus, and simply, no punishment for a short period of time. But I savored the reward, and he knew it.

One day, only a couple of months after the abuse started, he decided to introduce oral sex, cunnilingus, to be precise. This was more abhorrent to me than anything he had previously done to me. It was a repugnant intimacy that left me feeling completely desolate. I felt soiled to the core of my being. When he finished, he laughed and wiped his mouth. Suddenly feeling defiant, I kicked him and ran to the bathroom to take a bath. I wanted to wash his every touch and every ounce of shame off of my body. But he followed me. He pulled my small frame out of the tub and dragged me, naked and kicking and screaming, back to the bedroom.

"Do you really think you can get rid of me that way?" he yelled. "You stupid shit! I'm not going anywhere, and neither are you. You better learn you are not allowed to leave until I say you can go."

He forced me to stand before him, still naked, shivering, while he leisurely smoked a cigarette. Then he masturbated until he ejaculated all over me. Finally, when he was sure he'd gotten his point across, he gave me permission to leave. It was easy to see how much pleasure he derived from humiliating me. It was so empowering to him that he literally "got off" on it.

My hatred of Ed was growing steadily. It was eating away at my heart. I tried not to think about him, about what he did. I tried to erase all the images he was putting in my mind. As children, we are able to do this some of the time. I believe it's because we are still so close to our spirit selves that we can find ways to block out the hate and the horror of our days for brief periods of time, time enough to reconnect with our souls.

Playing outside helped me be clearer, especially in the springtime. It was the only time I was free to be me. Nature always had a healing effect on me. It rejuvenated me and briefly soothed away the hurt I was feeling. Spring always gave me a sense of new beginnings and hope. As soon as the temperature rose above fifty degrees, I went outside barefoot to feel the grass between my toes. I played hopscotch on the cool cement or jumped rope with my sisters.

I noticed everything, from the sweet honeysuckle, where I would take the blossoms and suck out the honey, to the bees doing the same thing. I climbed the cherry trees and pretended I was one of the lovely pink flowers. I'd watch a robin feed her chicks and marvel at how trusting and insatiable they were. They would open their tiny beaks and allow their mother to put whatever she wanted into their mouths, trusting that she would give them exactly what they needed. In those brief periods, I could set my pain aside for a few moments.

Just like the baby robins, I trusted my mom. But eventually I began to wonder how she could allow a man to treat her and her children so badly. While she perhaps didn't know about the sexual abuse, she did witness his other mistreatment of us and, of course, experienced it herself firsthand. I forgave her because I craved her presence. I knew she was the only protection I had, even if her protection seemed to be dwindling away.

Although Mike never experienced the sexual abuse, he was emotionally and physically abused. Ed's favorite time to humiliate us was dinnertime. Eating was never pleasant in our family. Ed had strict rules. We were instructed to always keep our left hand under the table. It was never explained why, but if any of us failed to do this, our dinner was taken away and we were made to watch everyone else eat. One evening, when Mike put the ketchup on top of his potatoes instead of on the side of his plate, Ed threw his plate against the wall. "That's what putting ketchup on top of your potatoes looks like!" he screamed. "Shit!"

There was never any rhyme or reason to his rules. Everything he did was unpredictable. We never knew what the rules were, and if we disobeyed a rule, the consequences were swift and heavy. We learned fast, but there was always a new amendment popping up.

On the occasions when Ed ridiculed, humiliated, or threatened us in our mother's presence, she would do her best to divert his attention to herself. But he was not easily manipulated, and her attempts would only infuriate him more. Usually, he would attack her for defending us, and, as soon as he could, he would take it out on us privately. Mom didn't know this. She was essentially trapped in her own nightmare. She didn't make enough money to support us on her own, and I'm sure now that she believed there was no escape. She was weakened by her fear, which kept her bound to an abusive husband and kept her from protecting her children.

My only escape was the weekends I spent with my real father. He came back into our lives when I was eight, two years after he and my mother divorced, and we began to visit him every other weekend. However, after he remarried, these visits became sporadic because the woman he chose had three children of her own and was extremely jealous of our time with him. There were many times I wanted to tell Daddy what was happening to me, but fear kept me from saying anything. I feared not being believed, I feared he would blame me, I feared he would be ashamed of me. My time with him was too precious to take that risk. Being at his house was the only time I felt totally safe, and I didn't want to jeopardize that safety in any way. In my child's mind, I had somehow convinced myself that I would be rejected if the truth came out. I held my silence.

CHAPTER 4

Continuing the Cycle

One year turned into two, then three. My senses were numbed by the ongoing abuse. I was becoming anesthetized to Ed's assaults on me. I became more withdrawn and buried my feelings as deeply inside myself as I could, hoping maybe I could eliminate them completely. The isolation became familiar. There were times when my real father noticed my withdrawn behavior and asked if I was okay, but I just couldn't face telling him about what Ed was doing. I was too ashamed to talk about it. I thought I was somehow to blame for what was happening to me.

Each week, there were new humiliations to endure. I dreaded going home from school. One day, when my sisters had been invited to friends' houses, I was alone. Before I had a chance to change my clothes, Ed ordered me to his room, where he told me take off my clothes and go sit in the closet. I was terrified. This was something new. It was dark in the closet, but I could see there was a film projector set up in there. Ed came in, undid his pants, pulled out his penis, and turned on the projector. I sat in a fetal position, my knees pressed up against my chest, barely able to breathe. As the film began to roll, I saw images from every possible angle of a man and a woman having explicit sex. It was grotesque. I covered my eyes. He slapped my hands away from my face. "Watch it, goddammit!" he yelled. He grabbed my hand, rolled my fingers around his penis, put his hand around mine, and began manipulating it until he had satisfied himself.

That was when the film changed. Suddenly I was watching a man defecating. I cried out and buried my face in my knees. He pulled my hair, jerking my head back, "Look at the screen, goddammit!"

"I don't want to," I cried. "It's making me sick."

He turned on me, slapping me hard across the face. "You'll watch it, damn you, or I'll make you watch it ten times. Do you hear me?"

Crying harder now, I could only nod. I stared at the screen. I began to count inside my head, trying to keep the bile down. I turned my eyes, just barely, so he wouldn't notice, and stared at one of my mother's dresses. It was the pretty, red, polka-dotted one with the scooped neck and pleated skirt that swung when she walked. I loved that dress. I thought about the time I had put it on and twirled in front of the mirror. I thought about how grown up it made me feel. I wished I were grown up now so that I could go someplace far, far away from where I was at that moment. Finally, the film ended.

The physical trauma of that afternoon has faded now, but the memory still burns. A person who abuses children thinks nothing about the consequences of his actions, nor does he think of the emotional scars he leaves. He only thinks about the high. And the ultimate high for any abuser is *control.* Ed had control for six endless years.

When Mom, who could no longer deal with his abuse and controlling behavior, began to go out more and more with her girlfriends in the evenings, she left us home alone with Ed. I began to resent her absences. She was the only protection I had, and when she wasn't there, Ed's demands grew.

One night after we had all gone to bed, Ed woke me up and told me to come downstairs. It was a school night. I had been in a deep sleep, and I was disoriented. The butterflies began to circle in my stomach. He pulled out one of my mother's short negligees and told me to put it on. It was so big on me that it kept falling off my shoulders. I tried to hold it in place, but he slapped my hands away. I was too tired to argue. I stood there and waited for the next command. He lit a cigarette and stared at me without speaking, then handed me the lit Camel. "Here. Smoke it."

I shook my head. "I don't want to," I whispered shakily.

"I didn't ask you if you wanted to, did I? I told you to smoke it. Now do it!"

I took a puff without inhaling, but some of the smoke escaped down my throat and I began to choke.

He started to unzip his pants. "Since you can't seem to suck on that cigarette," he said sarcastically, "I'll give you something else to suck on."

This was the worst of all the things he demanded. Every time I had to do it, I would vomit. That night, however, just at the moment he was about to use force, he jumped up from his chair and ran to the window. He zipped up his pants, grabbed my pajamas, and jerked me up the stairs by the arm. I knew my mother had arrived home.

He shoved me into my room. "Put your pajamas back on," he hissed, "and you had better be asleep if your mother comes in here. Do you hear me?" His lips were tight, and I could see the veins popping out on his temples. My eyes on those veins, I didn't answer him. "Do you hear me?" he said again. "You better keep your fucking mouth shut, or I'll kill her," he said, spraying me with his spittle.

Those words got my attention. I ran for my bed and buried myself under the covers. Would he really kill my mother? What would happen to us if he did? The thought of living with him and without even the minimal protection we got from our mother was too much to think about. So I prayed. I begged God not to let that happen. I made a bargain with Him. I told Him I would let Ed do whatever he wanted if He would protect my mother.

And God gave me what I asked for.

It wasn't long before I found out that Ed had friends who were just like him. I can't remember how many times he took me to their houses to flaunt the power he had over me by humiliating me and fondling me in front of them. I look back now and wonder how he got away with it. I wonder how in God's name I endured it.

One incident comes to mind, I suppose because it was the last time he ever took me to someone's house. I believe I was eight years old. He told Mom he was going to the liquor store and I was going with him. I remember looking at my mother with pleading eyes, but she just gave me an encouraging nod. When Ed clutched the back of my neck, I knew I had no choice.

After Ed picked up his supply of booze and cigarettes, we pulled into the driveway of a small, run-down house. I could see we were in a very poor area of town. The butterflies began their dance in my stomach. I never knew what these situations would bring. My guard was up before Ed stopped the car.

Ed knocked at the door, and a man I'd never seen before answered. He was very tall, with black skin, a solemn face, and kind eyes. He said his name was Bill. He smiled at me, and what little comfort his kind eyes had given me vanished. Anyone who showed any kindness or interest toward me made me suspicious. All men had ulterior motives.

We stepped into Bill's living room, and I sat down across the room in a torn chair with plaid upholstery that made the backs of my legs itch. Ed pulled a bottle of scotch from the bag he'd brought in, and the two of them began drinking heavily. As the alcohol took effect, Ed started boasting about all the things he could do to me. He ordered me to come sit in his lap. I had to obey, though my face flamed in embarrassment as he openly fondled my chest.

I wasn't sure if it was the alcohol, but Ed seemed quite comfortable in Bill's presence and it made me wonder if this man behaved the same way Ed did. Ed took another gulp of his drink. "I'll let you have some of this," he said, reaching under my skirt to touch me. When I immediately clamped my legs together, Ed laughed. "You have to let me watch and take pictures, though."

I felt as if he had just punched me in the stomach. The blood drained from my face, and there was a knot in my gut that cut off my breath. Hoping to protect myself from a second blow, I wrapped my arms around myself.

Bill stared at me, and for a fleeting moment I thought I saw a flicker of anger . . . or was it compassion? Or sadness? I couldn't tell. I looked away. It must have been my imagination. When he spoke, it was very softly.

"Kids aren't my bag, man. It just ain't right." He shook his head and looked down at his shoes. "I think you need to go, man, and you need to get some fucking help. Jesus, she's a fucking kid, man."

Shocked by his words, I looked up at him, desperately wanting to believe him. Had he really said that?

Ed jumped up, and I fell off his lap. He jerked me to my feet. "Go get in the car!" he yelled. He turned on Bill. "Fuck you, man!" he said. "You told me you liked young chicks. That's why I brought her here."

"Young chicks don't mean eight-year-old girls, man. That's just sick."

I stood outside the screen door, listening.

Bill had more to say. "What you're doing is a crime, man. If you get caught, they're going to slap your ass in the slammer."

Those were the last words I heard. I ran to the car and waited.

In the darkness of the car I could hear myself breathe as I replayed in my mind what Bill had told Ed. My heart slowed its pace. *Could it be true? Was Ed committing a crime?* I wanted to believe it so much that a small smile flickered across my lips.

But the only positive thing that happened as a result of that experience was that Ed never took me to visit any of his friends again. He was scared. He knew he had taken a risk, and now he was afraid. He was beginning to lose control.

CHAPTER 5

The Power of Control

A child who loses control of his life can grow up wanting to control everything and everyone around him, usually through anger, guilt, jealousy, and possibly violence. These are all fear-based emotions. Another child may grow up feeling as though the only way to feel in control is to hold in her emotions to ensure herself that she is protected from feeling any pain ever again.

I took the latter route to deal with my pain. I held my every emotion in tight control. I was distrustful, insecure, and depressed. I lived in self-denial. By hanging on to negative thoughts, I could not see myself as a decent human being worthy of receiving love and capable of giving it.

As the abuse continued, I went deeper inside myself, but not to that lovely healing place that resides within each of us. I went into a dark corner of my mind so that I wouldn't have to look at anything. I was impure, tarnished by guilt and shame. I couldn't bear to look at myself. These feelings were very real, and there was no one to help me, no superhero to call upon for rescue, not even the slimmest hope of ever finding a hero. I knew the only person I could count on was myself. Knowing that I was all I had left me feeling completely desolate. My desolation slowly turned into anger, which led to my eventual rebellion.

A master at manipulation, Ed used his powers to control us children. If I wanted to go out after school, his response became, "You have to earn it. You're not worthy of that privilege until you show me."

I began to hear *You have to earn it* over and over again, and it was not only addressed to me, but to my sisters as well. That's when I began to realize I was not the only "victim." *You have to earn it* was Ed's code. The real message was, *There were no free passes before a performance.* It was always about what he wanted to do sexually to me (and my sisters) or what he wanted me (or them) to do sexually to him. He used this phrase many times in front of my mother, and she never knew the hidden meaning. He thought he was so clever with his code that he'd laugh when he said it. Ed needed to maintain control and feel more powerful.

One day comes to mind. We were going shopping with Mom. Ed came along, not because he wanted to, but so that he could monitor me and my sisters. I'm sure he lived with the constant fear that, given the opportunity, I would tell my mother what was going on. We passed a toy store, and in the window I saw the Thumbelina doll I had requested for Christmas that year but didn't get. She was the most beautiful doll I had ever seen. She looked just like a newborn baby, and I craved something to nurture, or perhaps it was just my desire to love something because the hatred I was feeling for myself and my stepfather was threatening to consume me. My birthday was coming up in a few weeks, so I pulled Mom aside and pointed to the doll. I begged her to get me the doll.

She was noncommittal. "We'll see, honey. She's awfully expensive."

I knew that meant I would never get the doll. Mom always reminded us of our financial state whenever we asked for something that was beyond her means.

A few days passed. I tried to forget about the doll. Then Ed called me into his bedroom after school. "Come over here and take off your pants. I want to eat you, and then you're going to do the same to me."

I stood in the door, and for the first time since the abuse had started I shook my head. "I don't want to," I told him, even though my voice was shaking. I'm not sure where the courage came from to say those words, but it felt damn good.

My small courage infuriated him, and before I knew what was happening, he had me pinned to the wall with an arm against my throat. With his other hand, he ripped off his belt and lashed me with it several times. The pain sliced through my clothes, and I cried out with every blow.

"I said, take off your clothes."

Defeated, I gave in. Turning my back to him, I slowly undressed. I couldn't stand the sight of him and didn't want to give him the satisfaction of seeing me cry. When I was naked he pushed me flat on the bed and masturbated until he ejaculated all over me. Then he jerked open the closet door and pushed me inside. "Get in there and stay there until I say you can come out." He slammed the door shut.

Sitting in the darkness, I pulled one of his shirts from a hanger and wiped myself with it. Then I wrapped one of Mom's blouses around my shoulders, tucked my knees up to my chest, and held myself. I rested my head on my knees and cried. In the darkness of my thoughts, I decided this small act of rebellion was worth the consequence of his actions, even though he had won.

When Ed returned, my tears had stopped. I was no longer fearful, merely resigned. He opened the door and told me to get up. "Get your ass dressed, you little bitch, and go downstairs and clean up the kitchen. I don't want to hear one fucking word come out of your mouth. Understand?"

I remained silent, but nodded. When I reached the bottom of the stairs and walked into the living room, I saw Dianna sitting on the couch playing with the Thumbelina doll I had asked for a few days before. My heart sank even lower. The packaging was strewn all over the floor, and she was wrapping the doll in a pink blanket. A fresh on-slaught of tears threatened, stinging the back of my eyes, and my chin began to quiver. Dianna looked up at me with a gloating smile. She had not asked for the doll, but she knew I had, and I'm sure that, on some level, it made her feel powerful and in control. I understand now that when you're a child and your world is a jumble of turmoil, pain, and humiliation, you want others to feel that pain, too. So Dianna was reveling in her brief moment of con-trol. Even then, on some level, I understood all of that. But I was only nine years old. I was hurt. I was angry at her for gloating.

This is exactly what Ed had sought to achieve. He gave me a self-satisfying, evil grin, then leaned over and whispered in my ear, "She earned it. Now go clean the fucking kitchen."

As soon as he said those words, my anger evaporated. It was all so sad. In that moment he confirmed my fear. *I was not the only one tangled in his web of abuse.* He had a hidden agenda. It was his desire to turn my sisters and me against each other. He knew that if he could achieve this, we wouldn't band together to tell our mother. I walked to the kitchen feeling dejected, numb, and much older than my nine years.

Although it took me many years to truly understand it, one of the things I began to see that day was the high some people get by having power over others. It's like an aphrodisiac to them. An abuser craves it. Power is an addiction. At some point in his life, Ed saw the effects of having power, most likely through his own experience of neglect or being emotionally, physically, or sexually abused by someone who had power over him. At an early age he learned that if you want to survive in this world, the only way to do so is by controlling others. He witnessed firsthand that the more power you have over someone else, the better it will make you feel. Undoubtedly, he also saw over time how power takes on a new force and becomes unmanageable. The more the abuser abuses, the more he wants to abuse, until eventually irreparable damage is done, not only to the person being abused, but to the abuser as well. He will end up getting caught, or he will destroy himself.

I've come to believe, however, that abusers have another choice: that is, to seek help. Sadly, many abusers don't believe they're doing anything wrong. They blame others. They justify their actions, and many who sexually abuse children have convinced themselves that children like what their abusers do to them. Abusers don't get that children's complacency is merely their fear manifested. Abusers allow the experiences of their own life to transform them, but what they are, are lost souls buried in the misery of their own anger and pain. They stay attached to the pain by living under the umbrella of the "poor me syndrome" or the anger they choose to hang on to. This pain is born out of fear. Ed lived a life of fear. First, he was afraid of his mother. Later, he was afraid he would lose control. Then he started to be afraid he would be caught. Maybe he was afraid he would go to jail. Or maybe he was just afraid that he would never have another chance to molest or hurt someone again.

I was a tiny, defenseless girl. Even as I was becoming a source of fear for him, I was also allowing my own set of fears to infiltrate my psyche. I believed what he told me. He taught me many fears, but they were different from his. I became afraid of darkness, afraid of men, and afraid to trust or to feel affection and love. But somewhere in the deep recesses of my mind I could hear the steady beat of my heart telling me I was strong, that I could get through this, that there would be light.

It was the voice of hope. Even though it was sometimes the barest whisper, it was always there.

As the months progressed, I began finding my strength.

The summer of my eleventh year was the beginning of the end. Ed was fired from his job. In addition to his excessive absenteeism, he had been caught stealing from the company he worked for. His fall into the abyss was not far off.

School was out for the summer. Ed was home all day. He became very demanding, and there was never a way to escape him. I was becoming more and more defiant. I was learning that no matter how painful the repercussions might be, disobeying Ed was worth the small bit of satisfaction I received. There was no doubt that he noticed my rebellious nature.

One Friday, I invited my friend Kristie to sleep over. Normally, I never invited anyone to my house because I didn't trust Ed, but Mom was going to be there on this particular night. That gave me a false sense of safety.

That night, Kristie and I were "camped out" in the living room in our sleeping bags. Ed and Mom had gone to bed hours before, and I had just fallen asleep when a movement in the dark startled me awake. Ed was kneeling down beside me. When I opened my eyes, he clamped his hand over my mouth and whispered, "Wake up your friend and have her pull her pants down. Tell her I want to eat her."

Shame and nausea washed over me. I started to sweat. If I did as he asked, it would mean not only the end of my friendship with Kristie but also the end of my life at school. It would mean my pretense of a normal life would be revealed for what it really was. I knew I couldn't bear the humiliation. School was the only refuge I had besides Daddy's house. Now Ed was going to destroy it. The hate

I felt for him began to boil inside me. I could feel it rise to the surface like rocket fuel for my courage. Not only was he asking me to hurt myself, but he was now asking me to hurt my friend. I was in no way prepared to do that. I shook my head.

He squeezed the back of my neck until I cried out in pain. Kristie woke up. Ed released me. She sat up and rubbed her eyes. "What's wrong?" she asked.

"Nothing," I told her. "It's okay."

Ed gave me a warning look. He had been drinking, and in his reckless desire to have what he wanted, he began to speak. "Amy wants to ask you something. Don't you?" He reached for my neck, ready to hurt me again.

Repulsed by his tobacco- and alcohol-tinged breath, I turned away. I looked at Kristie. "He wants you to do something dirty," I told her, "and I told him no. I told him I am going to tell my mother if he doesn't leave us alone."

If anger could be seen in the physical sense, I've no doubt I would have seen fire spewing from every pore in Ed's body. He stood up and took me with him. Sensing his rage, Kristie yelped. When she did this, he loosened his hold on my neck and grabbed my hair. "You are going to pay for this, you fucking little bitch." Seething, he turned and walked upstairs.

Kristie was crying. She wanted to call her mom. She wanted to go home. I managed to calm her down by promising her it was okay, nothing would happen. I told her just a little bit about my life, leaving out the awful details, and trusting that she would keep my secret. The next morning, when she called her mom as soon as breakfast was finished, I had the feeling I had lost a friend forever.

The rest of the weekend I managed to avoid Ed by staying close to Mom, but I knew, come Monday, he would swoop down on me for revenge.

Looking back on that day, I would have to say that that Monday was probably one of the worst days of my young life. I arrived at school and was welcomed by an onslaught of disdainful stares from my classmates. I was uneasy. Was this the result of what happened Friday night? Had Kristie told everyone about Ed? By lunchtime I could hear their whispers. No one would speak to me, so I sat alone. On the playground I became the target of ridicule. Yes, Kristie had told everyone. I was the object of scorn and judgment.

The jury had come back with a guilty verdict. It was my fault. They had determined that I was the one to blame. I tried to walk away from their hateful stares and sarcastic slurs, but they followed me around the playground, throwing pebbles at my back until one of the teachers told them to stop. It didn't matter. My body was numb, my spirit was broken, and I was so consumed with shame and guilt that I didn't even feel the rocks that hit me. I just wanted to run and hide. I hated myself so completely in that moment that it became a physical pain. Their voices faded into muffled taunts. All I could hear was my own voice crying out, "I want to die, I want to die, please let me die."

When I got off the bus that afternoon, I was in so much physical and emotional pain it was difficult to walk.

I knew Ed would be waiting to administer his own punishment, but I didn't care. My only hope was that in the
heat of his anger he would kill me. Then I wouldn't have
to feel anything ever again. Seconds after I reached our
house, Ed ordered me into his bedroom. The normal com-
bination of fear and nausea that usually descended was
absent. I felt hollow. I was in the void that comes when all
hope inside of you dies.

He ordered me to undress. I didn't fight him. I did as I
was told. "Stand up and look at me," he ordered. I did. The
stench of alcohol and cigarettes assailed me. He slapped
me hard across my face. "Don't you ever, ever disobey me
again. DO YOU HEAR ME?"

It was clear that he had been planning and savoring
the method of punishment he would use against me all
weekend, and his anger was just the first phase. "Answer
me, goddammit!"

I nodded.

"Good. Now lie down."

Again, I didn't argue. I lay there, waiting for the end.
He tied my hands and feet, then stood over me, stroking
himself until he ejaculated all over me. Then he turned
me over and began hitting me with his belt. I screamed
as each blow made its mark, but I refused to cry. When he
finished beating me, he pulled me to my feet and dragged
me, naked and broken, into the closet.

"See what a mess you've made of yourself?" he sneered.
"I'll come back when you've had time to think about it."

I welcomed the darkness. My backside throbbed in
pain. Standing there, I was able to loosen the cloth belt

that still bound my hands together. As usual, I pulled one of his shirts from a hanger to wipe away the mess he'd made all over me. While I usually felt some small measure of satisfaction at soiling something that belonged to him, this time I didn't feel anything. I threw it aside and sat down carefully, waiting for the pain to subside. When numbness began to set in, I sat down and rested my head on my arms. I tried very hard not to feel anything.

Ironically, I felt I had gotten off pretty easy. I somehow sensed behind his bravado that he had noticed my odd behavior. Maybe he was afraid that I would tell my mother. A small smile grew on my lips, but the victory was tiny. I knew I couldn't tell her. The risk was too great. Every negative outcome played in my head, rewinding itself over and over and over. What if she didn't believe me? What if she blamed me like my friends at school did? What if Ed killed her? As these thoughts crossed my mind, my fear turned into something else. My body began shaking with an overwhelming power, until finally I gave in to it and allowed the tears to fall.

"God!" I cried out. "Why me, God? Why is this happening? What have I done?" I kept asking the same questions. But no answers came. This silence from God validated what I believed: I had done something to deserve the bad things that were happening to me, and God wasn't going to talk to me until I figured it out and fixed it myself. In my mind, I wasn't even worthy of asking Him for help.

The pain of feeling deserted even by God rolled itself into a tight ball of unbearable shame. My friends were

right. I was now irrevocably convinced everything happening in my life was my fault. I figured that if God were
going to save me, He would have done it by now. I cried
and I cried until I thought there were no tears left in me.
And when Ed finally came in to dismiss me, I went to my
bed and wept some more.

When my mother came home, she came to my room
to check on me and I pretended to be asleep.

CHAPTER 6

My Test and Ed's Abyss

Even to this day, I am shocked by Ed's boldness and aggression toward my friend. Kristie was outside the boundary of his inner circle of abuse. Most pedophiles will only try to manipulate a child if they feel some kind of security in their environment, but by this time Ed's sickness was blinding him and he was living with a false sense of security. He thought he would never get caught, that he was somehow invincible.

But he was in a downward spiral, and very quickly things began to disintegrate between him and my mother. He was drinking heavily, and his violent side became exposed in ways I hadn't seen before. When my mother was home he directed his anger at her, both verbally and physically. When she wasn't there, it was directed at anyone in his path.

In the fall of my eleventh year, the financial burden on my mother had become too great for her to handle. Ed was still out of work and making no effort to find a job. As a result we were forced to sell our house. We moved into a small apartment in a poorer section of town. For me, this meant going to a new school, and for this one small blessing, I was thankful. It was a new beginning for me because no one at this school knew about my stepfather, and I had learned not to trust anyone ever again with information about my life. My classmates at my old school had never forgiven me for what my stepfather had tried with Kristie. Until my last day there, I remained an outcast. So I learned to keep my secrets to myself. My lack of trust resulted in my making only one friend, Pam, during the brief time I was at my new school.

But the move inflated Ed's anger because the close quarters of the apartment hindered his ability to have his way with me and my sisters.

Before the school year ended, my mother had filed for a divorce. She came home one afternoon and announced we would be moving to Florida as soon as school let out. The joy I felt must have been that of a prisoner being released from incarceration. The only sadness I felt was the prospect of not seeing Daddy every other weekend. When Mike asked Mom about this, she assured us we could visit him during holidays and in the summer.

As quickly as my joy arose, however, it was extinguished when Mom went on to explain that Ed would be taking care of us for the first two months in Florida while she stayed on in Indiana in order to earn the company car she had been driving.

I wanted to scream at her, tell her she couldn't do that, it wasn't fair, we needed her there to protect us. All I could do was cry.

Ed listened to my mother with his jaw clenched tight.

He wasn't happy about the impending divorce, nor about the move, but since he had neither money nor leverage, he was forced to go along with her plan. When I began to cry, he gave me one of his threatening looks. He knew why I was crying, and it made him furious.

Mom tried to console me. "It's okay, honey. It's only two months, and I'll be there before you know it." She believed my tears were coming from separation anxiety. In a sense, she was right. Her absence from me would give Ed free rein to behave any way he chose without interference from her or my father. For a brief, happy moment, I'd thought I was escaping from him. The truth was that Mom was sending me straight into the devil's pit. I wasn't sure if I could survive it.

Once school let out, we began packing our few belongings. It was only a couple more weeks before we would leave for Florida, and I was already feeling depressed at the prospect of spending my whole summer in a new place with no friends and Ed in charge of my life. I decided to walk over to my friend Pam's house, hoping she could cheer me up. She was my only friend and we had grown sort of close, though she never really knew anything about me.

I remember the day well. It was beautiful: the sun was high in the sky, beaming down through puffy, white clouds, and the birds were singing happily through the rustling leaves on the trees. I walked along the road, lifting my face to the breeze and absorbing the sounds of summer. Mother Nature was soothing me as she always did.

Being outside gave rare moments of freedom and happiness that I couldn't find anywhere else, and I could feel myself relax as I walked.

It was such a beautiful day, in fact, that I decided to take the long way around to my friend's house so I could enjoy the sunshine. Instead of cutting through yards as I usually did, I walked down the main road. The street was bordered with stately oak trees and towering maples. There were houses to my right, and to my left were the rolling hills of a lush green golf course. I thought about how I would never again ride my sled over those snow-covered hills and naively wondered if it snowed in Florida. Lost in my thoughts, I turned onto Pam's street. Her house, which sat high on a hilltop, was half a block in front of me.

As I rounded the corner, I saw a car pull up at the stop sign. The man inside the car rolled down his window. "Excuse me," he said, smiling at me. Feeling slightly uneasy, I stopped. He had dark hair and horn-rimmed glasses. I remember thinking there was something about his looks that reminded me of Ed. "Do you know where the Browns live?" he asked.

I felt immediate relief and allowed myself to trust this stranger. I knew the Browns. They lived directly across the street from Pam, and I was proud of myself for remembering that. "Yes," I said, pointing to their house. "They live right over there."

I could tell he was slightly surprised. He hadn't expected a positive answer. Brown was a common name, and I'm sure he had chosen it as part of his plan. That's when he opened his car door. "Hey, do you want to see something?"

Uneasy again, I backed away. Then I looked into his car and stood frozen in horrified silence. He was completely naked and playing with the bulging mass between his legs. Seeing my panicked expression, he reached out to grab me. I bolted. My heart was in my throat. I couldn't breathe. I ran straight ahead as fast as I could toward Pam's house. I looked back once and saw him make a U-turn. I managed to reach the driveway and ran up the hill to her back door. I knocked as hard as I could, but no one answered. There was no car in their driveway! No one was home. Why hadn't I called first?

I peered around the porch, hoping he'd driven away. He was still there! He saw me. I ducked down behind a corner of the porch, my heart pounding so hard I could hear it. I didn't know what to do. I began to cry. I prayed he would leave. Seconds passed, then I heard a car door open and shut. That's when I heard the voice inside my head say, *Run, Amy! Run as fast as you can!*

Without looking to see where he was, I jumped up and took off in the opposite direction, through the neighbor's yard. Cutting through more yards, passing barking dogs, and running through the woods, I finally reached my own house. I ran inside and slammed the door behind me. Leaning against it for support, I took a big gulp of air and felt my heart rate begin to slow down, but I was shaking so hard I had to sit down on the floor before my knees buckled under me.

I couldn't believe what had just happened. *Why me?* I asked myself. *Why me?* I leaned my head against the wall and closed my eyes. *It was my fault.* I blamed myself for taking the long road, and not my usual route, I blamed myself for speaking to a stranger, something that girls were told not to do, even in the sixties. I even blamed myself for being pretty. If I were ugly, I told myself, he never would have stopped. I convinced myself again it was all my fault. It's amazing how far the ego will go.

I never spoke of the incident to anyone. I had this perpetual and undiluted fear of not being believed. I was sure that everyone would somehow come to the same conclusion I had—*I was to blame for all of the bad things that were happening to me.*

Today, however, looking back on my childhood, I look at that incident as one of many tests I was given as a child so I could develop into the person I am today. My test on this occasion was *trust*. As children, we are taught to trust our parents and adults in general. However, it's unusual to be taught to trust our feelings. My first instinct was that there was something wrong with this man, but I allowed myself to believe what I was taught: when an adult asks you something, you answer politely. I had trusted that this man was a "nice" man who was only seeking directions.

Children who are abused have their trust continually tested. "My mother beats up on me, but I should trust that it's okay." "My uncle sexually abuses me, but I should trust that he loves me." "My parents verbally abuse me, but I should trust that their words are true." These are all tests in trust.

It's interesting to learn the original meaning of the word *test*. It is derived from the Latin word *testum*. In the Middle Ages, *testum* became the word for the evaluation of precious metals in a shallow, porous cup, the *cupel*. When impure silver or gold was heated in the *cupel*, impurities in the metal were absorbed in the porous material, leaving a button of relatively pure silver or gold. The metal had been *tested*. By the sixteenth century, *test* was also being used figuratively. To "put something to the test," or to "bring something to the test," was to make trial of it, to determine its quality or genuineness, as a precious metal was tested in the *cupel*.

If we bring this concept of testing into our lives today, we can say we are all being tested daily. We are all trying to determine what our quality is, learning how to find our genuineness, because we don't know about the precious metal that resides inside us. Our souls are our *cupels*, helping us to melt away the impurities of our lives so that we may see the golden beauty within us.

If I had known then what I know now, I wouldn't have beaten myself up. I would have remembered the vibrant green leaves that rustled in the wind that day. They change into crimson and gold and eventually fall to the ground, where they will be mulched into the soil and fed to the tree of life. They rest in winter and by spring will provide nutrients for the new leaves.

The human life cycle is much the same. We have tests; we make choices. Sometimes our choices cause us great pain and we need to rest to regain our strength. But the real beauty of our tests is not whether we pass or fail. It's coming to the understanding that all tests appear in our lives to help us find the beauty that was always there, sometimes hidden, but always there waiting to be revealed in its purest form. It is understanding that we don't fail our tests; they are lessons that help us discover the truth of pure gold that lies within each of us after the impurities have been melted out.

CHAPTER 7

The Beginning of the End

It was late June when we packed up the car to leave for Florida. We drove down the highway in a thunderstorm. How fitting it was, I thought, that the weather echoed my own turbulent feelings. I was still angry at my mother for making us go with Ed. I didn't care if she got her stupid car. It was more important for her to be with us. However, somewhere in the unreachable space within me, I convinced myself she was doing what she thought was best for all of us.

It was a two-day trip, and as we got closer to our destination my anxiety mounted. Pretty soon, Ed was going to have the freedom he craved to behave any way he chose.

When we arrived at what was to be our new home, my heart sank. We rode down a street lined with shoddy duplexes, where garbage, broken furniture, and beat-up cars decorated the driveways. I kept hoping Ed had made a wrong turn and we were in the wrong neighborhood. Then we pulled into a driveway. This couldn't be it! Ed had the wrong house. My mother would never have chosen a place like this for us to live. This wasn't at all what she had described to us. We sat in the driveway looking at faded stucco with splotches of gray where the paint had fallen off from constant exposure to the sun. I looked at the sand in the small space that made up the front yard. It was filled with weeds and prickly burr plants. I got out of the car and walked around to the back, looking for a patch of green grass. All I saw was a larger version of the front. Where was the beach?

To my dismay, the inside of the duplex was worse. There was a small living and eating area with a tiny galley kitchen jutting off behind it. Since Mom was bringing our furniture down in a U-Haul truck, she had rented the duplex furnished, but the furniture looked like something someone had pulled off the street we had just driven down—a faded green, threadbare sofa, a small, rickety coffee table, a wooden kitchen table with four plastic chairs. There were three bedrooms, one for Ed, one for Mike, and one for me and my three sisters. The only furnishings in each bedroom were mattresses on the floor. This alarmed me enormously, because everywhere I looked I saw dead cockroaches. They were on the floor and in the kitchen. And, worse, there were families of them still living in the cupboards. I looked at Mike and then at Dianna and Lindsay and saw reflections of my horror on their faces.

I was transported back to the small, dark duplex we had lived in before Mom had married Ed. This seemed much, much worse. At least back then, there were no cockroaches, we hadn't had Ed to contend with, and at that innocent age I had still believed in God. I had believed He was a loving, protecting God. Now, at age twelve, I had become cynical. I looked around the depressing bedroom and thought how selective God must be. Because apparently, it didn't matter how sorry you were or how many times you asked for forgiveness. If you weren't on God's A-list, then you didn't have a chance.

A couple of weeks passed and I managed to avoid Ed's advances by pretending to be sick or staying close to Mike. It didn't occur to me that the smaller living space would make it more difficult for Ed to achieve his desires with discretion.

Mike became my real savior, my angel without even knowing he was. We all disliked our new home and missed our mother and our visits to our father, but Mike was becoming increasingly desperate. He finally decided to call Daddy. He wanted to tell him about our living conditions. Once he described how things were for us, he said, Daddy would surely rescue us. It was about three weeks after we'd arrived when Mike walked up to the nearby 7-Eleven and made the collect call to our father. He cried on the phone as he told him about the house and how unhappy we all were. He begged Daddy to come get us.

Hanging up the phone, Mike ran home and gestured for me and my sisters to come outside, away from Ed. He was gleaming with excitement. We walked around to the side of the house so that Ed wouldn't hear us. What was going on?

"I called Dad," Mike whispered, "and I told him how bad it is here, and he's coming to get us. Can you believe it? I knew he would . . . I just knew he would," he repeated as if he really couldn't believe it himself.

His excitement was contagious. I couldn't quite believe

it, either, but this was the validation I needed. Mike loved me enough to call our father, and Daddy loved me enough to rescue me. It immediately released the fears I was having about never seeing Daddy again. My fear was not that he wouldn't want to see us; it was the influence Audrey, his second wife, had over him. Over the years I had witnessed the jealousy she felt for us and our mother. When Audrey and my father married, she had one son and two daughters from a man who had abandoned her and her children some years before. My father had immediately adopted her children, and he and Audrey soon had a son of their own. We loved our half brother and stepsiblings and looked forward to our times together, but there were many times when I also felt Audrey's hostility toward us. She begrudged the time we had with our father. She begrudged any money he spent on us or gave to my mother for support. This became a source of contention between my father and her, and they would fight openly about it.

Every year before school started, for example, Audrey would take her kids shopping for clothes. Sometimes my sisters and I would be at their house. I admired all the things she bought my stepsisters and thought how exciting it must be for them to have so many beautiful new clothes for school. Since money was tight for my mother, one outfit and one new pair of shoes was all she could afford for each of us, and we were happy to get that much. As I stood listening to Mike assuring us that Daddy was coming to pick us up, memories of one particular incident involving Audrey came flooding back.

My sisters and I had gone shopping with Audrey and her daughters to buy them clothes for the new school year. When we returned, my father was watching a ball game. My stepsisters plopped their shopping bags down in front of him and began pulling out item after item of clothing to show him. He looked over at me and my sisters. We were sitting quietly on the couch. When he realized that we had nothing to show him, his jaw tightened. That's when he asked Audrey, "What did you buy *my* daughters?"

Audrey's temper flared immediately at his reference to *his* daughters. She lit into him. Pointing at her own daughters, she said, "They're your daughters, too!" She pointed at my sisters and me. "Their mother can buy them their own goddamn clothes with the money you give her."

Daddy gave her a warning look, but he didn't say anything. A minute later, he stomped off to the bedroom, and she followed right behind him to finish what she had to say. I could hear her screaming at my father and him screaming back at her. He would not, he yelled, allow her to treat us differently. When we were with him, we were to get the same treatment as the rest. He was my hero that day, but when he came out of the bedroom, all I saw on his face was defeat. That evening when he dropped us back home, he handed our mother some money and told her to buy us some school clothes with it. That became the routine every year. It was his way of avoiding arguments with Audrey. I never knew how much he gave our mother. We still only got one outfit and one pair of shoes. She needed that money for other things.

Even though Mike had told us our father was coming for us, I was uncertain as to how Audrey would handle the fact that we might be staying in her home for a while. I wondered if she and my father had argued about it.

But I felt so proud that Daddy was coming all the way from Indiana to rescue us. When he arrived, I could sense that he was proud of himself as well. He had followed his instincts and trusted that what my brother had told him was true. He had immediately gone out and bought a brand-new Chevrolet station wagon so that we would all fit in the car.

When they arrived, we kids were all waiting outside. Daddy and Audrey stepped out of their shiny new car, and we ran over to hug them. (That day happened so long ago, and yet it feels like yesterday.) After a few minutes of joy, though, my father turned serious. I'm sure he was thinking of the confrontation with Ed that lay before him. He reached in the back, pulled out a camera, and asked Mike, "Which house is it?"

My brother pointed to it.

"Is Ed there?"

Mike nodded apprehensively.

Mike opened the front door and we followed my father into the small living room. Ed was seated at the wooden table, which was covered with empty beer cans and overflowing ashtrays. It was only noon and he was drinking his umpteenth beer of the day and smoking a cigarette. When he saw our father, he looked up and nervously put out his cigarette, but he stayed seated. The look of fear on his face was a magical moment for me, so much so that, to my own self-disgust, I almost felt sorry for him. Clearly, he thought that the unexpected visit was due to my sisters and me ratting him out, and he was scared.

My father looked straight at Ed. "Mike called me and told me about the living conditions here. So I came to see for myself."

My father's disgust became evident as he walked around the duplex and took picture after picture of the squalor. He came back to Ed.

"What the hell were you and Eve thinking? Tell her I'm taking the kids back to Indiana with me, and I'll be filing for custody."

My father was a tall, burly man with a thick reddish beard and sparkling blue eyes. When he smiled you could see the diastema, or gap, between his two front teeth, the same gap my older sister inherited from him. But he wasn't smiling now. The expression on his face dared Ed to try and stop him.

Daddy quickly moved from room to room again, taking photo after photo. "Kids, pack some things." He looked at Ed with barely concealed rage. He had seen enough. He was furious at my mother for sending his children to Florida to live in a place like this with a man who was obviously a good-for-nothing drunk and completely incapable of taking care of five children, four of whom were his. "Kids, get in the car *now*. I'll be out in a minute."

I looked over at my little sister, Susie, who was Ed's daughter and five years old at the time. She looked confused and sad, and I wanted desperately for her to come with us. I couldn't bear the thought of leaving her behind with Ed. "Can Susie go with us?" I whispered to my father.

"I'm afraid not, sweetie," he answered regretfully. "Now go get in the car."

Even though I was happy to be going with him, my heart was breaking that we had to leave Susie behind. I had never considered her to be just a half sister. She was my sister, totally and completely, and I wanted desperately to protect her.

I went out to the car and started crying. "What's wrong, honey?" Audrey asked. She had a Tennessee twang that reminded me of country music singers, and she was being so nice to us today that I felt a little confused.

"Nothing," I said. "I just wish we didn't have to leave Susie here with him."

"I know. I'm sure your father would like to take her, too, if he could, but she don't belong to him. He could get into trouble for doing that."

As we piled into the car, I heard Daddy tell Audrey how he hated leaving Susie behind. He said he had been only seconds away from taking her, too. The gratitude and love I felt for him at that moment nearly overwhelmed me. Here was a man, an only child of divorced parents, who had so much compassion for children, not just his, but all children. He had four of his own, had adopted Audrey's three, had one with her, and then said he would have taken Susie, too. He gave with his whole heart and soul without ever blinking an eye.

The trip back to Indiana became a family vacation. We stopped in Orlando to visit Marineland and stayed in a hotel with a pool where we could swim after dinner. The previous three weeks of living in a roach-infested house with a drunken pedophile quickly became a blur from the past. Visions of the future dominated my thoughts as Daddy explained that we could all live with him if we wanted to. He told us how he was going to finish off the basement and turn it into three bedrooms. It sounded like a dream come true. God had finally answered my prayers. Audrey seemed especially enthusiastic at the prospect of us living with them. I still found this very curious. Her past behavior suggested that she would not be pleased about the possibility of her stepchildren moving in, but I tried not to think about that and focused instead on her enthusiasm.

When we arrived at my father's house back in Indiana, we were greeted by our stepsisters and -brothers. For two days we talked about the possibility of us all staying and how much fun it would be for us to go to school together. It would be just like the Brady Bunch. But at night, I would lie awake thinking about my mother and how hurt she was going to be if we all chose to stay here. All she would have would be Susie. Then I thought about Susie being alone with no one to play with her. I thought about Susie being alone with Ed.

I felt so torn. I wanted to please my father and stay with him. After all he had done, I felt I owed him that. He had driven all the way to Florida to rescue us. How could I betray him? What kind of gratitude would that be? But my heartstrings kept tugging at me until I finally came to the conclusion that maybe he wouldn't be angry because he would still have Dianna, Lindsay, and Mike, plus my stepsiblings. He could do without an eighth mouth to feed, especially when Mom would need me so much.

A week after we returned to Daddy and Audrey's house, Mom showed up, distraught and crying. It had taken her a couple of days to convince her boss to let her go early and still keep the car. When he finally agreed, she drove to Daddy's house to get us.

She didn't know that we'd already made some plans. Dianna and Lindsay had decided to stay. Mike was going to drive back to Florida to help our mom and then return to Indiana. I'll always remember that night. Mom was crying, my sisters and brother looked remorseful, Daddy was neutral, and Audrey's motives were finally revealed.

I walked over to Daddy and told him I was sorry, but that I needed to go with my mother and that Susie needed me, too. The pain I felt was unbearable and I started to cry. I could see that he was hurt, too, but he hugged me and said, "It's okay, baby. I knew you'd go back, and I love you for that." His understanding made me feel better, but there was still some guilt attached to my heart.

When I went to say good-bye to Audrey, she gave me a hard look and pulled me close to whisper in my ear. "You don't know how much you just hurt your dad. Out of all you kids, he wanted you to stay the most."

Her words cut me to the core, and a new surge of tears filled my eyes. How could I ever forgive myself for hurting the one person in my life who had never done anything to hurt me? It was as if I had stuck a knife into the only person who truly loved me. Later, I realized that Audrey wanted all of us to stay because she knew how much it would hurt our mother. She was insanely jealous of Mom, and her jealousy led to a visible hatred. I realize now all of her emotions stemmed from her own inner anger and fear that she wasn't good enough.

I allowed Audrey's words to create another layer of guilt that took me a very long time to peel away. First, I had hurt Daddy. Second, I didn't want my brother and sisters to think I was favored over them. Deep down, I knew it wasn't true. Daddy loved all of us. But it took me many years to overcome the culpability Audrey's words made me feel.

CHAPTER 8

Breaking Free

Today when I look back at those events, I feel a deep sense of admiration for my father for doing something that must have been very difficult for him at the time. His compassion and love for us were immense. I always felt that his determination came in some way from his own repressed feelings. He had endured an empty childhood, and he was not going to repeat the errors of his own father and mother. He had taken responsibility for his children with a steadfast devotion that still inspires me.

I left my father that long-ago day carrying a heavy load of guilt. I was twelve years old, but I felt ancient and alone. My mind was full of turmoil and doubt. One part of me felt good for making the decision to go with my mother, but the other part criticized me mercilessly for choosing to go back to a life of abuse, even though I knew the end was near. Mom had said Ed would be leaving and was only staying with us until she arrived and he could find a job and afford to move out. Mom told us this on the way back to Florida. I couldn't believe it! God was playing a cruel joke on me. The chances of Ed looking for a job while he was still being supported by my mother were slim to none. In the meantime, he would be free to continue his abuse.

As we got closer to that awful duplex, I felt a determination that I had never felt before. By the time we arrived, I had made a solemn vow to myself. *I would never let Ed touch me again.* Somehow, I was going to take control of the situation. He could scream at me, threaten me, beat me, but the only way he would have his way with me again was over (or upon) my dead body. As far as I was concerned, there was nothing left to lose except my soul, and I knew he couldn't take that away from me, no matter what he did.

I kept that promise to myself. My life became a living hell for the six months he remained with us, but the feeling of pride was worth the price of enduring that hell.

Mom started her new job shortly after we arrived. School had not yet started, so I was left to contend with Ed on my own. I looked for signs that he had abused Susie while I was gone, but couldn't see any. For that, I was very thankful.

The very day my mother started her new job, Ed called me into his bedroom. He wanted to know what I had told my father.

"Nothing," I replied defiantly.

His look indicated he didn't believe me, and he pressed me on it. "Someone must have said something to him, or he wouldn't have come down here and whisked your asses away like that."

"I didn't say anything to my real daddy about you. He came down here because Mike told him about this house and how bad it is."

Ed was grinding his teeth. A sign of rage. He hated it when we used the words *real daddy,* and he heard the defiance in my voice. From the moment he and my mother had married, he had forced us to call him Dad, something none of us wanted to do. But we were given no other choice. His expression now turned ominous. He reached out and squeezed my face between his fingers. "You better cut the attitude shit," he said, "or I'm gonna make your life a living hell. Now take off your clothes." He pushed me at the bed. "I want some pussy." The look of dark, sexual anticipation crept over his face. It was the look that always caused my stomach to churn.

My insides turned into Jell-O, but I stood still and shook my head.

"What the fuck do you mean? Get your ass over here. Now."

"I don't want to." I took a step back and tried to stop my voice from quivering. "I don't want you to touch me anymore. I don't want to touch you."

His face got so red it looked like he was going to explode.

I continued. "I'm going to tell my mother if—"

Before I could finish, he had me pinned against the wall, his hands around my throat. It was as if all the anger he had suppressed had finally geysered out. I could barely breathe.

"Now you listen to me," he sputtered, "and you listen good, you little bitch. If you tell anyone, let me repeat, *anyone,* I'm going to kill you. But first I'll kill your mother, and it'll be *your fault.* Do you understand me? And then

I will kill you, you fucking little bitch." He squeezed harder and I choked. "So don't threaten me. You got that?"

Unable to move, I stared up at him. I was sure my neck was going to snap. He finally released the pressure just enough for me to take a breath.

"Do you understand me?" he bellowed.

I nodded. My courage was evaporating fast. He looked like a crazed animal, and I knew that he was capable of carrying out his threat. I just wasn't prepared to challenge him.

Finally he released me, and, to my surprise, he pushed me out into the hall. "Get out of here before I beat the shit out of you!" He slammed the door behind me.

My relief was unspeakable. I rubbed my neck and wondered why he had let me go. Although I was still shaking, I allowed myself a small moment of victory. Was he afraid of something?

I learned something about power that day. It was an enlightening experience, but the most gratifying thing of all was the feeling that I had taken back a small measure of control over my life, control that Ed had held captive for so many years.

CHAPTER 9

Letting Go of Control

Control is a powerful tool. When used to cripple an individual emotionally, it can have lasting effects, especially in children. A child controlled through intimidation grows up feeling insecure, not knowing quite who she is because she has been told all her life to behave a certain way and usually in a way that does not naturally define her real self. She has not been free to develop her own personality. I only use *she* as an example. Boys who are abused experience the same kind of trauma.

My stepfather had complete control over me for so long that I became his robot. When he said, for example, "Take off your clothes and lie down," "Take off your clothes and go into the closet," or "Take off your clothes and smoke this cigarette while I play with you," I obeyed him. I did what he told me to do, not because I wanted to, but because my fear was stronger than I was. Ed used my fear of him to control my every move. When he told me to smoke a cigarette and I tried to refuse, he'd threaten to make me smoke three. Fear won. When he demanded that I perform some perverted act and I refused, he'd make me perform two more. Fear won again.

It always did. My choices were not my own. I had to do everything he demanded because fear had been successfully ingrained into my psyche. I was a child who had no control over my actions.

Even in families with no history of abuse, controlling the children can take many forms. It may be subtle. The parent will often feel he or she is not harming the child. Control becomes harmful, not when a parent teaches a child to, say, look both ways before crossing the street; but when control hinders the child's self-development, then it becomes abusive.

For example, I once knew a family in which the father was militarily strict. They had four children, whom the wife homeschooled for religious reasons. The parents said it was to "protect them from the disgraces of society." The family attended church twice a week and considered themselves devout Evangelical Christians. To an outsider, this family might seem to be merely "protective." The children were well mannered, obedient, and never disrespectful. So, you ask, what's wrong with that?

What's wrong is that the only way those "good parents" were able to achieve this type of compliance in their children was through extreme measures of control, oppression, manipulation, and fear. This extreme level of control is what it took to turn four children into exactly what the parents wanted them to be instead of allowing them to be their own selves or permitting their personalities to shine through naturally.

The list of techniques of control used by the parents was endless. From the time they were babies, the children were told to always use the words *sir* and *ma'am* when addressing their parents or other adults; if they forgot, they were punished. Their freedom to socialize on a normal level was severely limited and never without the scrutiny or preapproval of the child they chose to play with as well as scrutiny of the child's parents. The children were disciplined for expressing any opinion that wasn't the same as their parents' opinion. They were ridiculed and humiliated in front of others for displaying any sort of resentment or hurt feelings as a result of that opposite opinion. For using a tone of voice that wasn't "agreeable," for example, they were interrogated and coerced into asking forgiveness—berated and beaten down until they confessed they had been wrong to use that tone of voice. They were taught to obey and accept everything their parents said as truth and never given a chance to speak their own minds. If they defied one word that was directed at them, they were physically and emotionally punished. I witnessed an incident in which one of the children was put down for crying because she didn't want lunch at the scheduled time. She wasn't hungry, having finished breakfast less than two hours before.

The children were taught about God, but their family's God was an angry God, one to be feared. They were taught that to be received by God or to receive God's love, you had to abide by the words of the Bible, but only as the parents interpreted those words. The children were taught that God is fear. He will only love you if you are good and fear Him. The parents succeeded in instilling this fear by telling their children they would go to hell if they were bad or if they refused to listen to their parents.

I witnessed this behavior because the parents were not afraid to show how well they could control their children. They didn't think what they were doing was wrong or that it was possible their actions could have a negative impact. Their egos were boosted by showing others how obedient their children were, how they dominated their family without any interference from the outside world. The power they had over their children made them feel proud.

The reality is that this kind of open abuse is somehow protected by a misconception: if there are no physical signs of brutality, then it's okay—it's not *real* abuse. Their egos convinced those parents that since they were church-going Christians, their actions were justified and society would protect them. Sadly, they were right.

But who's protecting the children? The suffering of the children in this family, although not as extreme physically as it was emotionally, was clearly evident. The lost, empty look in their eyes, their expressions of fear and uncertainty when their parents were present, could not be mistaken. I had the opportunity to come to the children's defense on several occasions. I felt it was my duty, especially since the parents chose to flaunt their abuse in front of me.

On one of those occasions, some years later, they were staying with my husband and me. I was standing in the living room when their oldest child, Amber, came in to say good night. Amber's mother asked her if she'd said her prayers. Amber responded with a sigh and said yes. It was this sigh plus her tone of voice that her mother didn't like.

It infuriated her mother and caused her to immediately bring the father in to discipline the girl. In my opinion, the best way to handle this kind of situation is simply to tell the child not to use that tone of voice and give her daughter the reasons why she didn't like it.

Instead, both parents took her upstairs and began to interrogate her. They wanted to know why she had used that tone and demanded that she ask for forgiveness from them and from God. I could hear everything that was going on because they were in the room next to mine. At the time, Amber was about fourteen and had started to rebel, so, believing she hadn't done anything wrong, she refused to ask for forgiveness. This further infuriated her parents. They began screaming at her and threatening to beat her if she didn't *repent.* I could hear her crying and screaming back at them, repeatedly asking why she had to apologize and *repent* when she hadn't done anything wrong.

They kept her in their room for nearly an hour, trying to break her down. When that didn't work, her father hit her. That's when I decided to intervene. I knocked on the door and walked in.

"What's going on?" I asked.

"This is none of your business," the father said. "Amber is our child."

"It's my business when you choose to abuse your daughter in my house."

I further told them that I was considering calling the police if they didn't stop. This was very awkward because they were guests in my home, but I was so mad, I didn't care. I told them their behavior was unacceptable and I would not tolerate that kind of abuse in my home. They let Amber go back to bed. The next day I tried talking with Amber's mother about their method of trying to get their children to behave in a certain way through fear and how in my opinion it could have damaging effects on them. But she cited the Bible to me and told me it wasn't her way, it was God's way. There was no getting through to her. They left that afternoon, and I never saw them again.

Discipline is a good tool when it's used with loving intention and not for the purpose of controlling another in order to feel powerful or better about yourself. Giving loving guidance to your children does not humiliate them. It shows them you care about how they behave because you want them to be the best people they can be. You want your children to see that by behaving in a proper way, they gain love and respect for themselves.

We need to tune in to our children's personalities and encourage them to grow through love and compassion, not control and fear. Love, not fear, gives them the freedom to explore and express their feelings. When we teach through love, if a child misbehaves, we don't correct the behavior by screaming, humiliating, or striking the child. That will only teach her what kinds of (negative) actions are acceptable. Instead, if we can take a minute to calm ourselves and firmly let the child know that it's not him we are angry at, but his behavior, then he'll learn more quickly. Even when siblings fight, we can ask them to recognize that when they hurt their brother or sister, they hurt themselves, too. Deep down, most children do feel bad when they lash out at a sibling or other person.

Children learn at a very early age that control is a survival technique they want to master. A toddler will show that she's learning lessons in control early in her development. She will spill her milk on purpose and give you a challenging look. She is not purposely trying your patience. She is looking for you to show her that no matter how she behaves you will still love her.

It's in these moments that we need to look more carefully at our children and try to see the spirit within them. Most children who misbehave are only looking for validation that you will always love them no matter what they do. If we can stop and position our thoughts in line with our spirit and take a look at the personalities of our children and understand what their needs are, then we will be successful.

A child will learn more quickly if taught with love, compassion, and humility instead of through fear, detachment, and superiority. Controlling a child to any extreme leaves that child feeling lost and dismayed at the world around him. But if we allow our children to grow with a sense of independence and the freedom to be themselves, with our loving guidance, then we will see them blossom with a sense of confidence and joy.

CHAPTER 10

My Turbulent Teens

I began seventh grade in September of 1972. I wasn't doing well in my classes, partly because I felt alienated and partly because of the stress at home. With my sisters living with our father, all the pressure was on me to give Ed what he wanted. Every day after school, he demanded that I go into his bedroom. Every day, I refused. Ever since that time when I'd threatened to tell my mother, he had decided it wasn't worth the risk to force me, though he still tried to persuade me. I was amazed at how easy it suddenly was to deny him.

His fear was now greater than my fear. As a result, he made my life more and more horrific. I dreaded going home after school. At first, he would just bully me. He'd slap me or jab me with his elbow as he walked by me. He'd push me into a wall and sarcastically say, "Excuse me." He'd casually brush his cigarette across my arm or leg and pretend that burning me was accidental. His verbal abuse was more scathing. He would make lewd remarks and call me a whore. He would tell me everything that had happened was my fault. He would say I had loved every second of his abuse. I tried to ignore him. Sometimes it worked. Other times, when he'd had lots to drink, he wouldn't allow me to ignore him. He would pin me to the wall with his elbow and fondle me, still suggesting that I liked it. Sometimes I could fight him off, but other times I only had to look at him with steely eyes and tell him to let me go or I would call the police.

Finally, after seven months that I thought would never end, Ed moved out, leaving destruction that took me many years to repair. I felt as though pieces of myself had been torn out and thrown away. I knew that I had to find a way to become whole again.

The first emotion I felt when he left was elation. Even though at times I was still afraid and thought it was too good to be true, I was finally free. The truth was that, on a physical level, I was safe from being abused again by Ed. *But he was still there in my mind.* I found myself moving from one living hell into another. The only difference was that the new hell was the one I created for myself.

I continued to blame myself. This had serious side effects on my life. My teen years were full of hills and bumps and curves and crashes that I created. My anger erupted unpredictably and in full force and was directed at anyone in my path.

Mom quickly remarried, but her new husband was only a few steps above Ed. Although he wasn't a pedophile, he drank heavily, and his dark side soon came out. I became angry at my mother for marrying men I thought were worthless. My anger at Ed intensified as I obsessively blamed him for stealing my childhood.

But the worst of my anger was directed at myself.

I had allowed the abuse to happen. *I* had not fought back. If I had, I would have learned sooner that fighting back worked. Even though the reality was that I had been a defenseless child, trapped in a horrible situation, I belittled and reprimanded myself constantly for being stupid and weak.

By age thirteen, I began hanging out with kids who did drugs. The first time someone offered me a joint, my initial reaction was to say no. But I quickly learned you can't say no and continue to hang out with the same group of kids. I finally gave in. The kids convinced me the joint would make me feel good, and *I really wanted to feel good.* I started with marijuana. For a while that worked. It helped me forget the pain of the past. When someone handed me amphetamines and barbiturates, I took those, too—anything to further erase the memories. Then came cocaine, the drug that numbed my senses from head to toe. When the high ended, however, it left a nagging in the back of my mind. It was a small, still voice telling me to stop or I would destroy myself. I listened with one ear and continued to do drugs.

When I was fourteen years old, I met a man named Keith. This was my first consensual relationship with a man. I was totally infatuated and drawn to his sense of childish humor. Little did I know that I was moving into another very controlling relationship. Keith was ten years older than I was, and he also had a two-year-old daughter. I met him in the park near my house, where he was playing with his daughter. A friend of mine introduced us; I began babysitting his daughter, and infatuation struck. He was flirtatious and funny, and by the time I was fifteen, a full-fledged relationship had developed.

He was the first man I ever willingly allowed to touch me. It was very difficult at first, but my feelings were also very different. I allowed myself to trust him. Soon I fell deeply in love with him. At least I thought it was love, but even then I had fleeting thoughts that my love was slightly misplaced. Perhaps I saw him more as a father figure than a boyfriend, but I ignored my misgivings and allowed myself to sink deeper and deeper into my infatuation. He was fun and made me laugh. He also made me feel like a grown-up. I remembered being a child and wanting so much to grow up, so this felt good.

At first things were great. Then a darker side to Keith's character began to appear. After several months of our love affair, he became domineering and insanely jealous. He accused me of looking at other men while we were dining out and dragged me out of restaurants. He expected us to get married and had a deep-seated fear that I would leave him once I turned eighteen. I tried to reassure him by telling him I wanted only him, but his imagination would inevitably set him off again, and he'd do something else to embarrass and humiliate me.

Then one day my sister Dianna got mad at me and blurted out to Mom that I had a boyfriend who was almost twice my age. Since I was only fifteen, Mom naturally flipped out. She told me I could never see Keith again. When I ignored her, she had a restraining order put on him and threatened to have him arrested for statutory rape if he didn't stay away from me. This enraged me—

how ironic this was, I thought, when she had never protected me from a much worse situation. I wanted to blurt out the whole sordid story about Ed, but, again, my fear and shame stopped me.

When Keith was served with papers, he became very paranoid. He decided to move to Fort Lauderdale, about twenty miles away, where he could keep a low profile, but he also wanted us to continue seeing each other. This new situation created more insecurity for him, and within weeks he was constantly questioning my whereabouts.

At sixteen, I began a waitress job in a restaurant, working evenings. That's where I found my very first "best friend," Michelle. She was two years older than me and encouraged me to go out to bars with her after the restaurant closed. Living in southern Florida had some advantages. Back then, you could go to bars with a fake ID and get in. Soon I was going out with Michelle on a regular basis. The first time I went, I told Keith, but he became so angry it frightened me. He forbade me to go out with her again and made me promise I wouldn't. But my promises only led to lies. I didn't want to give up my nights out with Michelle (we were having too much fun), but I didn't want Keith to find out, either, so I'd lie to him when he asked if I went home after work. With the restraining order in place, he couldn't call at home, and he wasn't supposed to come within a one-mile radius of my house. Given his controlling nature, I'm sure it must have been frustrating for him because he had no way of checking up on me.

But not long after Keith forbade me to see Michelle,

he became increasingly obsessed and began parking down the street from my house, waiting for me to come home. He was taking a risk and breaking the law because he was within a mile of my house. The first time he caught me, his rage took me unawares. He screamed at me and shook me so hard I thought my neck was going to snap. For the first time, I was glad I had the safety of my home to go to.

But I couldn't bring myself to break it off with him. I was afraid of how he would react, and there was another part of me that felt some kind of psychological dependence on him. As I look back now, I see that I also felt a sense of loyalty and devotion to Keith because he was the first man I'd ever given myself to. I'd convinced myself that I truly loved him.

But that summer, life threw me another curve ball. I went to the beach with my mother and new stepfather, along with one of my friends. We were in Fort Lauderdale, visiting my aunt and uncle, who were staying at a hotel on the beach. My girlfriend, Kim, and I spent the day on the beach, and as soon as the sun went down we headed over to the hotel pool to swim. There was a group of college guys from New York there, and they engaged us in conversation. They were all older, fun-loving, and good-looking.

We'd been chatting for a couple of hours when Dave, one of the guys, asked me to go for a walk on the beach with him. At first, I was hesitant and looked to Kim for approval. She encouraged me to go, which led me to believe it was a harmless situation. I wanted to believe it, too, because we were having so much fun. So I went with Dave.

It didn't take me long to discover I had put myself

in a very compromising situation. We walked down the beach and sat down in front of a cabana. It was secluded, which made me increasingly uneasy. I didn't want to sit down, but Dave promised we'd leave in a few minutes and assured me he just wanted to look at the ocean for a moment. Even though I sensed he was talking to me to help me relax, I remained tense. Moments later he began kissing me. I tried not to panic. I thought I could stop him. I told him I had to go and tried to break away, but he wouldn't listen. His kissing became more urgent. Soon his hands were moving all over me, pulling me down when I tried to stand up and run. Within seconds, he had my swimsuit off and was on top of me. Crying and begging him to stop, I fought him, but he was too far gone. He was six foot two and I barely weighed a hundred pounds. I was powerless to stop him as he entered me.

When he finished, he offered to walk me back to the hotel. It was as if nothing had happened, as if I had consented to his assault. I was devastated. I knew I could never tell my mother what had happened. It was my fault! I had willingly gone with Dave, even though my intuition had warned me not to, so the blame was mine. This wasn't rational thinking, of course, but as I played back in my mind what had just happened, I knew it didn't make any difference that he hadn't listened to my pleas and had resorted to force. *It was my fault.* I had encouraged him merely by being there. He was just a man who couldn't control himself. That was my logic. So I did everything I could to pull myself together. I vowed never to tell a soul what had happened to me, not even Kim.

But that vow was blown away when two and half months later, I vomited and passed out at work. My mother took me to the doctor. I was pregnant. She automatically assumed the baby was Keith's, and so did he. I knew it wasn't his because we had only been together once that month and he had used protection. I had never told either of them about the rape. I had buried that secret because I was afraid neither of them would ever believe me. I also knew that Keith would chalk it up to what he had frequently accused me of, my *promiscuous behavior*. Even though that wasn't the case, it's funny how we can accept the words and judgments of others. In Keith's jealous mind that's who I was—a promiscuous woman—and now I had come to believe he was right.

My mother persuaded me to get an abortion. She said it was the right thing to do. She reminded me that she had gotten pregnant with Mike at sixteen, and it had changed her life forever. I was worn out and too weak to think about it. I just wanted someone else to make the decision for me. I gave in.

The procedure was a success in the sense that I was no longer pregnant, but my body reacted with a vengeance. Three days later, I snuck over to Keith's house. We had dinner and were watching TV when I began to feel sick and feverish. I went to the bathroom and began passing clots of blood. I became dizzy and within minutes was losing so much blood that I began shivering. Keith panicked. He had no idea what to do, so he just took me home. But because of the restraining order, he dropped me off at the end of the street so that no one would see us together.

I was barely able to walk. My stomach was cramping and blood seemed to be pouring out of me. When I reached my house, I was thankful no one was home. By the time I got through the door, I was doubled over with pain and my pants were soaked with blood. I staggered into the bathroom and took my bloody clothes off and put on a nightgown; then I wrapped a towel around myself to absorb the blood that was still flooding out of me. I somehow got into my bedroom and lay on my bed, curled in a fetal position as the pain ripped through me. I was icy cold, paralyzed with fear and pain. Within minutes the sheets were soaked. I was shivering uncontrollably as my body fought the shock of losing so much blood. I pulled the covers over my body to hide the blood and stop the shivering.

Somewhere in the blur of my pain, I knew I was bleeding to death. A fog settled over me and I began to pray. I prayed for God to forgive me for taking the life of an unborn child, for I was sure this was the reason why this was happening to me. I prayed for Him to take away the pain. I promised to be good if He did. I prayed for another chance and cried out that I wasn't ready to die. Then I passed out.

When I awoke the next morning I was still weak, and the towel I had wrapped around me had crusted over. It stuck like dried mud to my legs. But I was alive! I was light headed and pale, but I was alive. I couldn't believe it. It was a surreal moment, and I felt as if I had dreamt the night before. Instinctively I knew a miracle had occurred. God had given me another chance to live. Tears welled in my eyes as I silently thanked Him. I was unworthy of such a gift. Even though I believed it was miracle, I was still too immature to understand the enormity of what had happened to me.

Then the fear crept back in. What if I wasn't able to keep up my end of the bargain? What if I screwed up again? What if I made another stupid mistake? Would God be so forgiving again? I had serious doubts that He would, and thus my overwhelming fear of angering Him took root. I tried to convince myself that it was really just luck that I had survived. God would never take an interest in someone like me. He never had before.

I rolled up the blood-soaked sheets and towels, put them in a garbage bag, and took them out to the trash can so that my mother would not ask questions. Fear was still controlling my behavior.

Soon afterward, I got on birth control and desperately tried to put the rape and the abortion behind me, along with my fear that God would retaliate if I sinned again.

CHAPTER 11

The Value of Trust

I was seventeen now. I continued to muddle through my turbulent teens, searching for freedom and my sense of self. But these remained beyond my reach.

Unable to keep a decent job and stressed out by the restraining order, Keith moved back to his home in Dallas, Texas. This gave me a huge amount of freedom. It was a relief to know that I no longer had to look over my shoulder and wonder if he were following me. I no longer had to wonder when he would show up to drag me out of a bar or scream at me in front of my friends. I no longer had a man telling me to change my clothes because what I was wearing would attract men. I no longer had to listen to a man who fed my insecurities by telling me, "You're going to get fat if you eat everything on your plate."

Keith's jealousy and mistrust impelled him to call me constantly from Texas and quiz me on my whereabouts and who I was with. Afraid that I was looking for someone to replace him, he interrogated me about other men. It's true that at first I didn't see anyone. I didn't want to betray him. I tried to reassure him and kept telling him I had feelings only for him and that as soon as I graduated from high school I would move to Dallas to be with him, just like we'd planned. He wanted to get married. I thought that was what I wanted, too.

Meanwhile, my mother encouraged me to date other men, and Michelle was also constantly trying to fix me up. Mom knew I was still in contact with Keith, and both she and Michelle wanted me to end my relationship with him so that I could enjoy what was left of my teenage years. But I clung to the ideology of getting married to Keith and starting a family, so I could have something to call my own. I had convinced myself that marriage would make everything right and my insecurities would vanish.

As a result of the bad choices I was making, however, my insecurities began to manifest themselves. First, I started overeating. Keith was no longer around to control the way I looked or criticize me for gaining a pound or two. He wasn't there to finish the food on my plate so that I wouldn't eat it. He wasn't there to look at me in disgust. But being overweight made me feel worse, so I went to the opposite extreme. To lose the weight, I began snorting cocaine and popping black beauties. Soon I was below my average weight.

The year after I graduated from high school (and one year after Keith had moved to Texas), I finally agreed to go out on a date with one of the bartenders from the club Michelle and I frequented. I was eighteen and enjoying my freedom. The love I felt for Keith seemed to be fading, even though we still spoke at least once a week and talked about our plans for the future. Although I was still stuck on the idea that Keith and I belonged together, I was having fun dating. Deep down, my heart was telling me to let go, but my mind refused to listen. After several months had passed I knew I had to go to Dallas and find out if we still had something. Keith had convinced me we did, so much to my mother's disappointment, I headed to Texas.

I landed a job working for a prominent law firm as a receptionist and law librarian. I was lucky because I didn't have any experience, but they were willing to train me. Having a professional job made me feel like a grown-up for the first time in my life. But bad omens began arising almost immediately. The first one came when Keith refused to give me a key to our small studio apartment. His excuse was that he hadn't gotten around to having a second key made. I suspected it was really his lack of trust. He didn't want me to have access to the apartment when he wasn't there.

Six months after my arrival, on a cold night in December with a light snow beginning to fall, I rode the bus home and walked the two blocks to our building. Keith wasn't there. Since I still didn't have a key, I was locked out. I waited on the front porch for nearly an hour until it finally got too cold and I had to ask neighbors if I could wait in the warmth of their apartment.

At 11:00 p.m., Keith finally showed up. I was furious and embarrassed at having imposed on our neighbors for so long, but he laughed it off with an apology and a vague excuse that he'd forgotten I didn't have a key. When we walked into the apartment, however, I noticed immediately that the bed I had made up before leaving for work that morning was now a rumpled mess. When I questioned him, he told me he had come home earlier in the day and taken a nap. Although I avoided a confrontation at that moment, this was the first time I actually listened to my intuition. It was sending me a message, and the message was loud and clear: *he was lying.*

Not long after that, an old friend of his dropped by unexpectedly. Before opening the door, Keith asked who it was. When his college buddy, Joe, identified himself, Keith told me to go sit in the bathroom until he could get rid of him. I understood his order. I had been around Joe before. He was a very attractive man who had openly flirted with me on more than one occasion. He'd even asked me what I was doing with a loser like Keith. I never told Keith this, of course, but Keith quickly picked up on the fact that Joe was showing a little too much interest in me. Thus he sent me to the bathroom to wait until he was gone.

But a few minutes turned into an hour, then two hours. Instead of defying his wishes, as I truly wanted to, I sat there, waiting and fuming and making my plans to leave him. Sitting alone in the bathroom, I knew that this was not the way I wanted to live my life. *I did not deserve this kind of behavior.*

A week later, I told Keith I was going home for the holidays. I was too afraid of what his reaction would be if I told him I was leaving for good, so I added that I would be back. Because of his uncontrollable temper, I avoided any confrontation. Three weeks later, I wrote him a Dear John letter expressing all my doubts about our so-called relationship and my desire to experience other things. He married someone else three months later. I was devastated.

Even though I knew leaving Keith was the right thing to do, his marriage was very difficult for me. It was the end of an affair with one man that had lasted most of my teenage years. I had given up the days of my youth to be with an older man. But as I look back, I realize that he taught me many things that I'm still grateful for today.

He taught me the value of trust. During my childhood, I had learned from Ed not to trust men. When I met Keith, I trusted him, but I also learned what it felt like not to *be* trusted by someone. It's easy to see now that his distrust in me was not a result of anything I had done, but a manifestation of his own insecurities about women and himself. Because I was young and naive and wanted his trust desperately, however, I never questioned his insecurities. I realize now that being with him helped me understand the nature of distrust and how it's something we create because we're afraid of losing something. I doubt that I would have learned that lesson without knowing what it's like to be on the receiving end of someone's distrust. I know now how much better it feels to be seen as honest and worthy of someone's trust. Much later in life, I realized that I needed to break my own patterns of accepting men who wanted to control me. This pattern had started with Ed and repeated itself with every man I dated until I finally came to understand what I was doing.

I also learned that love is not always what it seems. It wears many false faces. While I never doubted that Keith loved me, I now understand that his love was born out of a need to control something in his life. He didn't love me for who I was, nor did he care to find out who I was. He wanted me to fit into his mold of perfection, and he wanted complete ownership of the finished product. When I managed to break free of his mold, I entered a new chapter in my life.

I stayed in Florida for a few more months, but there were too many bad memories there and I wanted a fresh start. I needed to figure out what I wanted to do with my life. Michelle had just taken a job working as a flight attendant for Continental Airlines, based in Houston. She called me and convinced me to move to Houston. The decision was made simpler when my father told me he was also moving to Houston. He and Audrey had separated, and he had taken a temporary job there. I was excited about spending time with him. It would be an opportunity to get to know him on a deeper level, something I had never really had a chance to do while growing up. A few weeks in the summer and shared moments with seven other siblings didn't allow for much time for us to be alone and talk. Now I would be the only one of his children in Houston.

So I packed up my Toyota Corolla and drove to Texas. I enrolled at the University of Houston and immediately found a good evening job as a waitress in an upscale restaurant at the Hilton Hotel. I was making good money and enjoying being single and spending time with my father. I felt like I was finally on the road to maturity.

I spent a lot of my spare time with Daddy. We shared dinners out and Sunday afternoons barbequing. I helped him get through the pain of his divorce from Audrey, and he helped me heal the guilt I had experienced as a child for leaving him. For the first time in my life, I felt God had given me a gift and I was thankful for that period I had with Daddy.

But the one thing I never discussed with him was the abuse from Ed. As irrational as it was, I was terrified that Daddy would somehow blame me. I knew he had an image of me that was very pure, and I just didn't want to tarnish it with the truth about my past. Most of all, it was the shame that kept me from talking about it. There was no way I could ever explain what Ed did to me. I could barely think about it without the images coming alive, as if it had happened just the day before. Every time I thought about Ed, the shame would once again roar through me like a tornado.

Then one evening in early November, one year after I'd settled in Houston, I received a call at work. It was from Tonya, one of my stepsisters. She was in Houston visiting my father. I was very busy and not allowed to receive phone calls at work, so I was rushed when I took the call.

"Hello?"

"Amy, it's Tonya." Her voice was strained and then there was silence.

"Tonya? What is it? What's going on? I'm really busy, and I'm not supposed to have phone calls."

Then a man's voice came on the line. He identified himself as Tim, Tonya's boyfriend.

I felt an eerie coldness sweep over me. "Yes? What's going on? What is it?"

"It's your dad," Tim said, his voice unsteady. "He's been in an accident. A car accident."

As I clutched the phone, an image of a white Corvette flashed across my mind. I knew it could be bad. "He's okay?" I asked. "Right?" I could hear the pleading in my own voice. "Where is he? Which hospital is—"

Tim interrupted me. "He didn't make it, Amy. I'm so sorry. His car hit a telephone pole—he was killed instantly."

I felt my knees buckle. I sank to floor. "Noooo . . . Oh, God, noooo," I screamed over and over again until finally another waiter and the manager came rushing to my side. They picked me up. People were staring, but I didn't care. I was filled with a pain so deep that nothing else was real, nothing mattered. God had taken my daddy, my angel, the only man who had ever protected me and truly loved me for who I was. I didn't understand why. *Why him? Why me? Why was God still punishing me? Why must all the good things in my life be tainted with bitterness?* These were the questions I wanted answers to. I wanted desperately to understand why good people died. Was it to punish the ones left behind, or was it just a simple act of fate?

At that time, I believed I was being punished. I became angry with God. If He was going to punish me, then, I was going to punish Him back! I didn't believe in fate, nor did I want to chalk this up to "God's will." I wanted a valid explanation. If God refused to give me one, then I would stop speaking to Him.

I was nineteen then. I couldn't feel God's gentle hand patting my head. I was too self-centered at the time to know that each of us is on our own unique path of learning, choosing, and feeling. When bad things happen to us, God is giving us an opportunity to accept and ascertain, to have faith and believe, to forgive and let go. God knows that is what we need to do to move forward in our growth and understand that life is just a playing field and the real world is with Him.

My father had had a tough life. Even though he came from a nonviolent past, he carried the weight of some heavy emotional baggage. He was an only child whose father was an alcoholic. His father and mother divorced when Daddy was only seven years old. His mother never fully recovered from the loss. She became an alcoholic, too, and laid a powerful burden on her son, expecting him to take care of her and support her habit. He had to grow up quickly, but he always had feelings of inadequacy because he could never please his mother. He had to find work at a young age, and when he didn't come home because he wanted to hang out with his friends, she would pile on the guilt and tell him he was just like his father. This guilt was reflected in his eyes every time he witnessed one of her binges. He carried his feelings of inadequacy into his marriages with my mother and Audrey. He told me during one of our dinners that he felt like a failure as a husband and a father.

We'd had one of these conversations only four days before his death. After trying, and failing, to reunite with Audrey a second time, Daddy was having a difficult time understanding where he'd gone wrong. He had done everything possible to save the marriage, but it just didn't work and he blamed himself. He was suffering deeply, and although I offered encouraging words, I didn't have the wisdom at that age to really help him. There was such a tiredness, such a sadness, about him that it broke my heart. I felt as if he were giving up on life. My intuition was trying to tell me more. I now believe my intuition was trying to prepare me for his departure.

I was just too young to pay attention. It wasn't until years later that I was able to understand why we lose a loved one. Without the fog of pain obscuring my view, now I can see that my father needed to go home to rejuvenate his soul. I believe that death happens so that we can take time to realign ourselves with God and once again feel the intense power of love and what it means.

I know Daddy is still with me in spirit. I believe our mentors in life become our angels in death and remain by our sides. His death taught me to appreciate life, no matter how difficult it can sometimes be. I came to believe that he was ready to leave this plane, and whether his death was an accident or even an unconscious move to depart from life, he is happy now.

CHAPTER 12

Defining Pain and Pleasure

I believe we all have our angels, some visible and living among us, some we cannot see. Our angels help us in many ways. Sometimes they come to us in times of crisis, saving us from a disaster about to happen. Sometimes they come in the form of messengers and tell us what we need to move forward. My father was a living angel in so many ways that thinking about him still fills me with gratitude. That's how angels are. Whether living among us or in the spiritual world, they have the power to touch the spirit within each of us, giving us miracles that make life livable and helping us remember that love reigns above all else.

This brings forth a troubling question. *Where are the angels for the battered and abused children of the world?*

The answer is—they are here. *We are their angels here on earth.* There are some angels in the spiritual form, but we are the angels in the physical form. We have to be! God is not letting these little children suffer; it's *people* who are allowing the suffering. God wants us to hurry up and understand this. He gave us free will so that we might see for ourselves that all children deserve to be protected from harm. He wants us to use our free will and say, "Enough is enough. We will no longer allow these things to happen to our children." God has given us the power and the knowledge to do this, but it's up to *us* to take action. We have to take the first step in being the angels for the children.

We must not be afraid to take abused and battered children out of harm's way and enclose them in protective arms. God is not going to reach down and snatch them up. He's waiting for us to learn how to take care of them, perhaps so that we might experience the joy of acting nobly, but, more important, so that the children can heal and learn what real love feels like.

This is a difficult task when we consider that most people haven't learned how to love themselves. How do we teach a child to love if we can't love ourselves on such a basic level? The first step is to *let go of fear*. The only thing holding us back is our own fear of not being lovable on some level or another.

Denying love to ourselves creates a kind of love sickness, a feeling of being deprived of love that penetrates our psyche in a way that alienates us from our spirit. Our spirit knows we are lovable and works to help us see this. Even a person who has never been abused may have had the experience of feeling unloved. Our spirits are crying for us to believe in ourselves. If we could just have a little faith in knowing that love is our greatest gift, our greatest learning tool, our greatest healer, then the world would be a different place. When we look down upon ourselves, we become frustrated and tend to take out our frustration on other people. When we deny love to ourselves, it creates an inability to show compassion to our fellow human beings. We begin to say to ourselves that no one deserves love, least of all me.

While learning how to love ourselves may be a daunting task, there are ways to achieve it. In my mind, the easiest way to is to stop separating ourselves from everyone else and realize that we all come from the same collective force, an energy that generates only love, compassion, and forgiveness.

You can learn to love yourself when you stop comparing yourself with others, when you know you are completely unique and have qualities no one else possesses, when you stop looking outside yourself for someone else to validate your greatness. You can learn to love yourself when you no longer pass judgment on others and see the beauty in forgiving those who judge you. You can learn to love yourself by giving and receiving compassion. Learning to be compassionate will automatically call compassion back to you. Love sickness can be healed in that moment of compassion when we see that all men, women, and children are deserving of our help and our love. Loving yourself makes you feel good; it brings awareness and allows you to give to others without fearing that you will lose something as a result.

The second step we can take to teach our children love is to release the fear of acknowledging that terrible things actually do happen to children. We need to acknowledge that in most cases it is a family member who is committing these horrendous acts. This can sometimes be the biggest obstacle to acknowledgment because we don't want to believe that a parent could ever do such a thing to his or her own child. Irrationally and sometimes fearfully, we link their acts with our own acts of punishment of our children, and that brings things a little too close for comfort. Thus, we convince ourselves that the abuse probably isn't as bad as it seems. We try to forget about it. Or worse, we find the act of abuse so incomprehensible that we choose to ignore it completely because it's just too gruesome to think about. Too many times, an abuser is never convicted, or if he is convicted, he gets off on lesser charges. In some cases, the child is even put back in the hands of the abuser. Sadly, this teaches the child that his life holds no value and he is not worthy of protection or love. This is the biggest crime of all. Too often, we hear about these children on the news. They were sent "home." They were murdered.

It is known that in many cases abused children prefer to go back to their parents or the environment they came from. Even though they are being abused and as much as they would like for it to stop, they still want to go back to what's familiar. This is mainly in cases of younger children who want to believe their parents really do love them. Their hopes are that it will stop. Teens on the other hand, usually want to run away or become suicidal when abuse continues. This is the phenomenon of pleasure and pain. Pleasure and pain are the references on which we base every action. We ask ourselves subconsciously, *will I feel pleasure or will I feel pain from what I am about to do?* Frequently we are more apt to resist pleasure than pain. The world is living proof of that theory.

The pleasure an abused child seeks is a simple pleasure: *it's one day without pain.*

Some of the emotions that cause adults pain are self-denial, anger, guilt, hatred, and jealousy. These emotions cause us to act in ways that are in direct conflict with who we are. When we feel these emotions, we may say hateful things, commit abuse or murder, even go to war against each other. Not only do the recipients of our actions feel pain, but we also create pain in ourselves. It's this kind of pain that damages our psyches.

Pleasure, on the other hand, brings us joy, forgiveness, compassion, spirituality, peace, and love. The pleasures in life come from the virtues of the soul. The pains come from the habits of the ego. This applies to everyone, not just a person who has been abused.

Exploring pleasure and pain may help us discover who we are and help us uncover the child's world of abuse. Pleasure and pain are the two reference points by which we and our children can become better or worse than we are. Pleasure and pain rule our actions, some to a greater degree, some to a lesser degree. The way we pursue or avoid pleasure or pain can define who we are. For instance, when we choose to hang on to pain and use it for the purpose of growth, we are serving ourselves well. However, when we choose to hang on to pain to justify our actions of hurting someone else, we will remain spiritually impeded and wounded. A good example of this is divorce. Usually there is one person in the relationship who does not want the divorce, and this causes them great anger and hurt. That anger is often taken out on the kids, or the kids are used as a weapon to get back at the parent who left. Thus everyone involved gets hurt, especially the children.

When an abused child grows up and hangs on to the pain of her past, this ensures that other negative reactions will follow. It becomes easier to hate, judge, or feel inadequate. We want to control or blame and lash out at others and ourselves.

There are ways of ensuring that this pain doesn't manifest into something that is going to make our lives worse. Most abused children have just never learned what it is. The world of the abused child is so clogged with pain that she might receive only brief glimpses, if any, of pleasure. And her reaction to pain only causes her more pain. If we can come to understand that pain plays a fundamental role in experiencing pleasure, our hearts can begin to open.

Understanding that *if we never experienced pain, we would not know what pleasure feels like* is very important. Knowing what pleasure feels like is a good measuring tool because we will always strive to experience the feeling over and over again and in many different ways. Pleasure brings us joy. Being joyful and living in pleasure is, I believe, our goal and our purpose for living.

Pain is fundamental in achieving this goal. But an abused child must learn this concept differently than a normal child does. For example, a child who accidentally burns himself on the stove feels the pain, but he is then comforted and treated by his mother or father. This care helps him heal from that pain and thus provides a sense of pleasure. A child whose parent sticks his hand on the burner as "an example" and then punishes the child for being care-less suffers the added trauma of intense emotional pain.

How or when do these children ever learn what plea-sure feels like? The answer is that some children will never experience pleasure. Or when they do, they won't even recognize it. They'll become distrustful. Many will follow the pain of the past into the future. This ensures that every negative emotion attached to that pain will surface over and over again, which prevents them from feeling any kind of pleasure at all. The pain may mani-fest itself as anger, hate, jealousy, or violence. Those who inflicted the pain may have been extremely judgmental or controlling, which means that judgment and control are what the children will learn. When they get a little bigger, they may blame or lash out at others because they were never able to do so when they were smaller for fear of further punishment.

But even in the midst of the emotional breakdown that follows abuse, there is still a beauty hidden in an abused child that begs to surface. The beauty that was stolen from abused children still exists. But to find any pleasure in life, the grown-up abused child must make a conscious effort to rediscover the beauty within and listen to the spirit that beckons him or her forward.

Yes, pleasure and pain go together. It's part of the uni-versal flow. It is how we perceive pleasure and pain, plus emotions associated with them, that will determine what sort of persons we become. If we can learn to take our pain with grace and with forgiveness, then we will have mastered what our spirits seek. Bearing the pain inflicted upon us in childhood and learning to forgive are necessary to achieve happiness. Understanding that our abusers are on their own path of learning and that we were a resource for them (or, if you will, an instrument) may help us move forward. Understanding that *we were not to blame* and that this was just a painful experience will also help us survive and thrive.

These can be appropriate ways of dealing with painful episodes of the past so that we can move into personal growth and a new realm of pleasure. It is through our pains and pleasures that we are able to grasp who we truly are, and once we achieve this comprehension, we can learn how to love who we are. If we can be thankful for every experience in our life and come to understand that both pain and pleasure are necessary events that help us evolve to a higher level of being, then we will reconnect with our spirit and help our children.

That development will help us in our everyday lives. If we bear the pain of the death of a loved one, for example, by understanding that their spirit lives on and that we will one day be reunited, this can lead to pleasure. We can also bear the pain of divorce by being thankful for the growth the relationship provided; we can bear the pain of sickness with a healthy point of view that leads to healing, which in turn leads to pleasure.

The fact of living on earth is that we will always have pains to endure in this lifetime, and some pains will be greater than others. Whether it's abuse, the death of a loved one, a life-threatening disease, a handicap, unemployment, or a relationship that has ended, learning how to cope through love, understanding, and forgiveness is the most powerful method of overcoming the pain the challenge brings. Allowing adversity to immobilize us will only deny us the gift of a harmonious life. If we don't face up to the need to rescue our children, we fail to provide them the protection and love that are essential for healing and nurturance, and we thereby fail to help them experience a pleasure every human being deserves.

CHAPTER 13

The Process of Healing

I know firsthand how growing up with pain early in life can call forth a whole new set of pains later in life. During my teenage years, my pain manifested itself in a number of ways: I became angry at my mother for not protecting me, I was distrustful of all men, I was jealous of women more attractive than me, I hated my stepfather to the point of fantasizing about his death—just to name a few things. Worst of all, I hated myself. Letting go of these feelings was not even in my realm of thinking.

As I got older, however, I came to understand that healing is a process and does not happen overnight. The first thing we have to do is realize that we are in pain. Then we must confront it. If we can take these two steps, then we can move toward letting it go. But many of us tend to push painful images and memories out of our minds or try to bury them completely. Confronting abuse is difficult, especially when we'd much rather forget about it. Although no one wants to dig up the ugliness of the past and take a cold, hard look at it, this sort of analysis is necessary for the healing process to begin.

Some of us may want to go so far as to confront the

person who committed the abuse. When we do this, we are also making that person take a look at what he or she has done. If the idea of facing that person is too daunting, however, perhaps you'll want to start like I did, with a letter. When you write to your abuser, tell that person how you feel now and how he or she made you feel then. Writing is often a good way to express your thoughts without interruption or conflict. Even if you end up throwing your letter into the trash or burning it, just by recording your thoughts you've taken a major step toward your own healing. Composing this letter is a form of catharsis; it purges or cleanses your emotions. If for some reason you can neither confront the person nor write a letter, then just say *I forgive you* aloud. The power of words is incredible, and just putting the thought of forgiveness—and the word itself—out into the universe will increase your level of peace. Through prayer, ask God for assistance in helping you to forgive. The Higher Source in our lives is always listening.

Talking about the abuse openly will help, too. Find someone trustworthy, someone who will listen—a therapist, a family member, or a friend. Tell them your feelings, but take it one step at a time. Unless it feels right, it's not necessary to pour all your waste on the table at once. Talking about the abuse will become easier with each bit you decide to share. You will find with time that you'll want to get it all out, as hard as that may be, and you will realize that it feels good to do so.

I didn't talk to anyone until I was twenty-two years old. I finally broke my silence to my friend Michelle. I was still living in Houston and had gone back to school to get my travel agent certification. I wanted to travel, and though Michelle had tried to convince me to become a flight attendant like herself, I knew that particular profession wasn't for me. Being a travel consultant had more appeal.

Michelle and I still shared an apartment, and one night while we were watching the evening news we saw a story about a man who had been arrested for child molestation and murder. Naturally, she was appalled by the story. That's when I decided to tell her my own story. It was a big step for me. My fear of rejection was much stronger than my courage, but she listened and offered comfort and understanding. I was astonished that she didn't judge me or reject me.

Talking to Michelle was a freeing experience. Although the healing took a long time, that small conversation with my trusted friend started me down my own path of healing. The key is to keep talking.

Michelle also opened the door for my sister Lindsay and me to talk. One night after the three of us went out together and had come back to our apartment, Michelle brought up the subject of abuse. She asked Lindsay and me if we'd ever talked about the abuse to each other. Initially, we both froze at the thought. Finally, we admitted that we had never spoken about it. This was a challenge for Michelle to understand, and I'm sure others may not understand, either. One would think that it would be easier to talk to a sibling who shared the same experience, but in truth it was much harder—for many reasons. First, the shame was too close to the surface. Lindsay knew the way things had happened. It made those experiences more vivid when we retold them to each other because many of the events I experienced were identical to what she went through. This commonality seemed to magnify the shame, making it hard even to look each other in the eye.

Another reason it was harder to talk with my sister was that although we had been through many of the same experiences and had buried the shame, there was guilt attached because we had never done anything for ourselves or each other. Although I wasn't sure how much Lindsay remembered, once the conversation began it became clear that many of the same things Ed had done to her, he also had done to me, but we had processed events differently. This didn't matter, however, because we found that finally talking about the abuse with each other brought us both relief and bonded us more closely together. We could finally say to each other, "It wasn't your fault. I never blamed you for anything."

Our quest to purge the negativity of the past ebbs and flows in all of us. I got married about a year after that conversation with my sister, but I could not bring myself to discuss my childhood with my new husband. I simply told him that my parents had divorced and I had gone through a series of bad stepfathers. I never elaborated and he never asked.

Getting married at that time, I realize now, was something I did for all the wrong reasons. For one, I thought this person would complete me. Second, I also wanted children and I thought he did, too. Third, I think that on a subconscious level I was looking for a father figure to give me the unconditional love I was always seeking.

Going into a relationship with those kinds of expectations doomed it from the beginning. Because I didn't think I was lovable, I constantly questioned his love for me. I assumed he wanted all the same things I wanted, including a family of our own. My constant questioning and false assumptions led to other discoveries. The first was that when a man has to constantly reassure you of his love, he will grow weary very quickly. The second thing I learned was that having children was never on his agenda, which is what led to the third revelation—that he was having an affair with one of my colleagues. What was odd was that I really didn't care. By that time, I knew I had made a mistake in marrying him. The only thing I felt was relief. We separated and three months later our divorce was final. The marriage had lasted exactly one year.

During my separation, I began seeing a man named Tom, who had been introduced to me by the owner of the travel agency I was managing. Friendship soon turned into a relationship. Tom was nine years older than I and ready to settle down and have children. He wanted to get married as soon as my divorce was final. While I wanted to get married, too, I began worrying that it was all happening too quickly. But I turned off my inner voice and agreed to marry him two months after my divorce became final. I had convinced myself that he loved me and that he would make a good father because, unlike me, he came from a stable background, and I desperately wanted stability in my life.

These were all valid reasons, and they did make for a good relationship in the beginning. But, there were warning signals that I ignored. For instance, when we were dating and Tom told me that he was an atheist, I convinced myself that that wouldn't be a problem. Even I, after all, had questioned whether there was a God. I told myself that I could change his mind about God and thought that once we had children he would see how important it was to believe in something. It seemed the older I got the more I believed that there truly was a God. Another big sign was that when I tried to bring up my past and tell him what had happened to me, he inevitably changed the subject. I don't blame him. He was uncomfortable with a topic that was so alien to him and his own upbringing. He just couldn't comprehend my history, and I think he wanted to preserve the image he had created of me—that I was perfect and my childhood had been a happy one like his. After a few attempts to tell him the truth, I decided it was probably better for our relationship to keep my past to myself.

It worked until just after our first anniversary. Tom had gotten laid off from his job in Houston. Since his family was living in Atlanta, we decided to make a new start there and moved to Atlanta after the birth of our first child, Megan. We stayed with his parents until she was nine months old. It was a difficult time, but Tom finally found a new job and we were able to move into an apartment of our own.

We hadn't been in our new place more than five months when I got the call from Lindsay about Ed. Ed had remarried for a second time since his divorce from my mother, and the woman he had chosen had two young girls. (The marriage before that had also been to a woman with young girls.) We were outraged. Lindsay and I knew that Ed was still out there, still abusing little girls, still getting away with it. Lindsay informed me that she had already spoken to a district attorney in Florida, and that's when she found out that Florida had a twenty-year statute of limitations on child molestation. This meant that anyone who committed this crime could be prosecuted up to twenty years later.

A detective was sent to Ed's house, and it was discovered that he was indeed molesting both girls. That led to his arrest and got the ball rolling for his trial. The district attorney wanted to know if I would testify. Without hesitation, I said yes, and so arrangements were made for me and my sisters to fly to Florida for the trial.

As you can imagine, this came as a big surprise to Tom, who knew nothing of my past. He was sitting in the room when I got the call from my sister, and when I hung up there was an awkward silence. He finally asked me what was going on, but the look on his face told me he really did not want to know. I explained that my stepfather was being prosecuted for child molestation and that my sisters and I had been asked to testify against him. I left the door open for any questions he might have, but he had none. Clearly, he did not want to know the circumstances of my childhood and how they related to the case against Ed. Nor did he want to know the details of this case. He simply asked when I was leaving, how long I would be away, and whether they were paying for my airplane ticket. I knew right then that he wanted me to keep the door to my past closed permanently and that it would be better for me if I obliged.

It was the night before the trial when I boarded the plane for Florida, my daughter in tow. The thought of seeing Ed again after fourteen years had my nerves on edge. I had been twelve when he'd finally left us and had not set eyes on him since. I didn't want to think about him now. I didn't want to think about what he must be thinking, how he'd look, how he would react to my testimony. I didn't want to think about him at all, because if I did, all those memories would come flooding back and I would be faced with all the ugliness of my past yet again.

My biggest fear, however, was that of the unknown. We had set the ball in motion to finally have our revenge, and I was terrified of what the impact would be.

CHAPTER 14

The Trial

When I arrived at the courthouse in Fort Lauderdale the next morning, the D.A. informed me he had already taken my sisters' statements, since they had come down the day before. He needed to take mine before the trial began. We went into another room, where he began to prepare me for what lay ahead. He was kind and patient as I told him my story, and he was able to help me get through it with relative ease. He then informed me that Dianna would testify separately and that that was a stipulation she had put in place. Dianna was denying that anything had happened to her. She would not be offering testimony that Ed had sexually molested her. I found this very sad and told the D.A. so. I believe that Dianna, being the oldest, probably had things done to her that Ed had not done to me, but she has never spoken of it and I doubt that she ever will. I understand. It's the shame and humiliation that prevent her from speaking. I sympathize with her. But I believe that by not talking about it, Dianna has created more shame and guilt for herself that she must now contend with.

The time had come for each of us to face the man who

had taught us to hate, the man who had stolen the beauty of our childhood innocence. When it was my turn to take the stand, my stomach was churning and my palms were sweating. I walked into a courtroom full of onlookers and the jury. I tried to look anywhere but at Ed, but it was impossible not to see his face. When I took the witness stand, he was sitting straight in front of me. I took the oath, sat down, and clasped my hands in my lap. My heart was beating like a snare drum in my chest. Our eyes locked.

The man who had done unspeakable things to my mind, body, and soul stared at me with eyes full of hatred. Those awful eyes were the only thing about him that seemed alive. His body looked thin and frail, and his hair was gray and had receded. The only thing that had remained the same about him was his behavior. He still found perverted pleasure in molesting little girls.

The first emotion I felt when I saw him was fear, but that quickly evaporated and was replaced by pity. As I looked at him and saw the arrogance still flourishing in his unstable mind, I knew that even here, even in a courtroom full of people waiting to hear the truth of child abuse, he had no remorse. His only emotion was anger at being discovered.

The first questions came and were relatively easy to answer. I stated my name and my relationship to the defendant. Then came the tough questions. I was asked to describe the "first event" in detail and was then asked about subsequent instances of abuse. Keeping my attention and my eyes focused solely on the prosecutor, I poured out my answers. Then the tears came, but my pride kept my eyes averted from Ed's. I stayed focused on the jury.

When it came time for the defense attorney to ask questions, I never wavered. The truth made it easy not to. All the while, I could feel Ed's steely gaze boring into me, waiting for me to turn my head and look at him. He was obviously hoping he could still intimidate me. His arrogance led him to believe that he somehow still had control over me. When both attorneys had finished, I finally did look at him. His jaw was tight and his eyes were burning with rage. I'm sure that, given the opportunity, he would have jumped over the table where he was sitting and killed me then and there.

Giving testimony against Ed was a surreal experience, but as I was leaving the courtroom that day, the emotions I felt were odd. I think I was expecting jubilation at finally having my revenge, but what I felt was more sadness than joy.

I knew the chances of Ed's receiving help while in jail were slim. I had asked the D.A. if there were programs designed to help incarcerated pedophiles. The D.A. shook his head but said all prisoners could request counseling. So what would happen when Ed was released? He was sentenced to serve nine years, but the D.A. indicated he would probably get out for "good behavior" before then. This concerned me because I knew that without any psychological counseling while in prison, the chances of his continuing the cycle of abuse when he was released would be very high. The conventional wisdom is that most pedophiles are incurable, even when they receive help.

That meant that Ed's chances were pretty much zero. He was now a throwaway in society.

My sadness wasn't so much for him, however, as it was for the future of any child he might come into contact with after his release from prison. This is why it's imperative that these people get help or are kept under a vigilant monitoring program. Here was a man who had committed unspeakable crimes against children. But what about the crimes committed against him when he was a child? Do we forget about that? Label it as irrelevant? If we do that, aren't we contributing to the crime?

For Ed to break free from his own vicious circle, he would need to be taught a new way to live. Being incarcerated was a temporary, but necessary, fix. And while it was true that he needed to be taught a lesson, the lesson needed to come in the form of psychological, spiritual, and emotional retracing. He needed to go back to the source of his own abused childhood and address the issues of his past. He would need help, help in rediscovering who he was and why. But most of all, he would need love.

If no one taught him the lessons he needed, then Ed would come back full circle to where he was before and society would be the one to pay. Again. As an abused child, he never received help, but we sure felt sorry for him. As an abuser, he received no help, either, and society footed the bill to contain him. Many people resent the fact that we have to pay that bill when it's he who has done the wrong. They say he should pay. We find all sorts of justifications as to why it shouldn't be our responsibility. How could we have known he was being abused? He's an adult, they say. He knows the difference between right and wrong. They say Social Services should have done their job better. The list goes on and on, but all the excuses in the world won't change the plain and simple truth. If we don't help Ed and people like him, they will never see the consequences of their actions and the cycle will continue.

Turning Ed in and seeing him convicted did not heal me. It didn't automatically take away the pain of my past. While my mind told me it was the right thing to do and I was justified, my heart told me I had only prolonged the moment until he was free to abuse again. Don't get me wrong—I believe to this day that he needed to be punished for what he did. He needed to be taken off the streets so that he couldn't continue molesting little girls.

But I also believe that for Ed to get over his perversion he was going to need help and there would never be any help offered to him—certainly not while he was in jail—nor was it very likely that he would ever seek help willingly. But it's while abusers are in jail that the process of reeducation needs to begin. That's where the temptation is removed from them. Being in jail is also a period when they have time to reflect and hopefully feel some kind of remorse. It's at this time that we have the greatest chance of succeeding in helping men like Ed understand that their actions were hurtful and damaging. It's when they're in jail that they can be led to find a way through the emotional trauma they may have experienced as children.

When I decided to write this book, I sat down with a well-known district attorney in the Atlanta area who has tried many cases of child abuse. He informed me that the general rule on sexual offenders is that when they are incarcerated they receive minimal help, if any. But he was quick to reassure me that upon their release they are put on parole. If they offend again—molest more little girls or boys while on parole—they will be put away for life. However, the D.A. also confirmed the conventional wisdom: that virtually all pedophiles are incurable.

So what happens when they come off parole? Do they feel like it's a green light to continue the same behavior? Do we have enough police officers to monitor every sex offender once they are back on the streets? It's true that men like Ed would be taking a great risk by choosing to continue molesting children, but the question becomes this: *Do we want to risk the life of that child he chooses to target?* Pedophiles are sick. To a certain degree, they have no control over their behavior.

Ed served eight of the nine years he was sentenced to and is living near Fort Lauderdale now. Florida is one of several states trying to get a law passed that requires sex offenders to wear global positioning system tracking devices. Tennessee and Louisiana currently require them for some offenders. Other states (twenty-eight to be exact) and communities are cracking down by requiring notification when a registered offender moves into a neighborhood. There are more than half a million sex offenders registered in the United States today who are required to report their whereabouts, in some cases for the rest of their lives. A national Web site dedicated to tracking these offenders was set up in July 2005 (www.sexcriminals.com); most states also provide information online regarding the whereabouts of sexual offenders living in specific communities and neighborhoods.

These are all measures that need to be taken to protect our children. They are certainly deterrents for child molesters. I remember my youngest sister, Susie, telling me about a time when she and her husband were looking for a house in Florida in a neighborhood they liked. Her husband knocked on a neighbor's door to find out more about the area. The man who answered the door asked my brother-in-law if he and Susie had any children, and when he said yes, the man confessed to being a convicted child molester. He told Susie's husband he was required by law to inform anyone who had children about his background.

I was proud of this anonymous man for confessing his crime as required by the law. I wonder if he had ever received help. I can only speculate, but in my opinion he had taken a giant step in breaking his own cycle. He admitted publicly to his crime and was steering clear of children. Maybe he did this only because the law required it. If so, his admission was motivated by fear of getting caught if he broke the law. My hope is that he was motivated by remorse and was making a true effort to break the cycle and be healed.

It's easier to harden your heart against a criminal than to look for methods of helping him. It's much easier to convince ourselves that abusers are beyond help, so why bother? Such thinking lets us off the hook.

But the reality is that we should find ways to help these individuals. Not only is it the humane thing to do, but if we do not provide help and support, they will continue to seek out our children.

CHAPTER 15

Finding Inner Peace

Testifying against the man who abused me took a lot of inner strength. I had done a terrific job of burying all the horrible memories, so to be able to tell my story to a jury, I had to resurrect those unspeakable memories and speak them out loud and in front of a room full of strangers. Once the trial was over, though, I went back to my "normal" life.

I had a husband and a daughter, both of whom I loved dearly. I had a decent home that gave me comfort and made me feel stable. I had a life that was completely different from my childhood. I had vowed that I would give my own children a "normal" life, so once the trial ended and I went home I made a promise to myself that I would not discuss the topic of abuse again. And when my husband never asked me about the trial or the outcome, I knew that, for the sake of my marriage, I had to bury the past once and for all. I convinced myself it was probably for the best for everyone, but most of all myself, if I just put it all behind me.

But of course it didn't work. At night I would lie in bed and the images would reappear and haunt me. I'd close my eyes tight, hoping to keep them at bay, but they were always there in the shadows. If I let my guard down for even a moment, memories and images would resurface. I had no power over them.

When I agreed to testify against Ed at his trial, two things motivated me. Revenge was first. Putting him away where he couldn't harm other children was second. Healing myself was not a part of the picture. I'd never really thought about healing myself. Instead, I chose to look outside myself for ways to feel better. I knew putting Ed in jail was the best thing for him, and I thought it would make me feel better, too. But knowing he was behind bars did not bring relief.

When Ed went to prison, I was sure the images that tormented me would go with him and I would be free. It took awhile for me to understand that although they would never go away, with time they would dull until they could no longer hurt me. It took awhile to realize they were a part of me, a part of my learning process in this life, something I could use later to guide my own actions. I didn't know then that I needed these memories. I also needed to learn how to keep them without feeling the pain that was attached to them. For that to happen, I needed to forgive myself.

And I needed to forgive Ed.

Forgiving ourselves is one of the hardest things we can do. Our ego will fight us every step of the way. The ego doesn't believe there is anything to forgive. We didn't do anything wrong, so what do we have to forgive ourselves for?

What we must forgive ourselves for is *blaming ourselves for the abuse.* Somewhere in our subconscious mind lies the belief that what happened to us was somehow our fault, that we deserved it. We believe we are unworthy or tainted because we've been abused. We may believe these things happened because God didn't care enough to pull us out. We may think He abandoned us in our darkest hour. This causes us to think we are bad; otherwise, He would have saved us. Thoughts like these lead us to dislike who we are. Holding on to them leaves us exposed to more pain and hinders our healing. What we must do is look in the mirror and say, "I am good! It was not my fault. I am worthy of living a happy life. I forgive myself."

Repeat this as many times as it takes for you to believe it.

The next step in healing is forgiving our abuser. This might feel almost impossible, but it's necessary for the healing to be complete. Say, "I forgive you for what you did to me." Just saying these words out loud is a big step. Even if you don't believe what you're saying, if you repeat them enough times, it still helps. It may be easier to envision the abuser as a small child caught up in his or her own nightmare of abuse. Picture him as a human being who was humiliated, beaten, or raped as a child. The sooner you are able to do this, the sooner you will be free and at peace with yourself.

Hanging on to pain is tiring. Hanging on is the ego telling us that if we do this long enough, others will feel sorry for us and then maybe they will take it away for us. It's also the ego giving us permission to do things we wouldn't naturally do, like hurting others or lashing out in anger at others. If we never forgive the abuser (or ourselves), and keep reminding ourselves of what happened and how bad it was, then we have an excuse to hurt, blame, hate, and abuse. It's a vicious circle that keeps us stuck and incapable of moving forward. The ego has somehow convinced us it's better to cling to old hurts than to forgive anyone.

But we have a choice! We can take the experience of abuse and let it eat away at our peace of mind and torment us until we become physically or mentally ill, or we can take the lesson of abuse and say that the experience does not define us as bad persons.

These are the choices.

What we have to do is find a way to move forward and become a better person because of our experience. Maybe that means showing up for our own kids or being kind in our relationships or simply being happy with who we are. *But we can't do any of these things unless we forgive first.*

We must resign ourselves to the fact that bad things happen in this world for reasons we may not understand. But we should look at all of life's experiences through a wider lens. I believe our sole/soul purpose here is to discover who we are through our experiences and learn how to embrace each and every one of these experiences with love and understanding. While this may be daunting for a person who was abused, it is a necessary element in the growth process.

If we could turn our pain inside out long enough to view the love that resides within each of us, this would make it easier to accept our experiences. I'm talking about the spirit within each of us that is full of love. It's our divine being, our soul, if you will, that wants us to learn how to be thankful for everything. So, you may ask, *why I should I be thankful for any bad experience?* The answer is that while bad experiences are traumatizing, they can define us in a positive way. You're here, you're alive, you have now, this very moment, to start recreating yourself and making a conscious choice to live in the moment and be joyful for what you have. If we use what we learn from a bad experience to grow, we can turn it into something more powerful, something that allows the inner child to shine and allows us to say to the abuser, "You can no longer hurt me."

If we don't make this move we will remain stuck, and hatred and anger will eventually win. As a result, our body may physically experience the effects of staying stuck, which may even manifest as cancer or some other illness. We have to move away from the past and begin living in the present moment. We have to rejoice that we are alive and have the power to make changes in our life. If we can live with joy and make the rest of our life experiences good ones, then we are fulfilling God's prayer for each of us. For that is our purpose—to feel good, to feel joy in the beauty of life, to not waste time dwelling on our pain or bathing ourselves in self-pity. Our purpose is to shower forgiveness and compassion on ourselves and others.

I forgave Ed just before he was released from prison.

I felt like I had to do that so that I could live in peace knowing he was free. I remember lying in bed wondering how I was going to achieve this while the painful memories were still finding their way back into my head. Instead of trying to shut them out, I decided to replace them with pictures of Ed as a fearful boy going through the same dreadful things he'd put me through. I said to that child, "I will forgive you because you were only doing what you were taught. I will forgive you because you never knew love. I will forgive you because it is what God would do."

And then I cried. The toxins of my childhood were slowly losing their power over me. It is in that moment when you are finally able to forgive that you will be freed. The images may remain, but the pain attached to them will dissipate.

After Ed was released from prison, I sent him the letter that you read at the beginning of this book. It was the most difficult letter I've ever written, and even though he never responded I felt better for having sent it. I didn't expect a response, though I wondered how he would feel as he read it. Would he misinterpret my words? Would he think that I had somehow given him permission to continue abusing because I had forgiven him? Would he gloat over the power he had had over me? I may never know. Maybe he just threw my letter away and never gave it another thought.

I finally stopped asking myself what his reaction would be because in the end it didn't matter. Ed is on his own journey. I took one giant step in my journey in trying to help him see that his actions had a negative impact on me and on him, but it's up to him now to move forward and make good choices for himself. He will have to change himself, with or without help. If he continues to abuse little girls, the consequence will be life imprisonment. And that's a decision he'll have to live with for the rest of his life.

CHAPTER 16

Using Prayer to Heal

Since I never went to church as a child, I never learned about prayer. I never learned about God or the Bible. I simply had an intuition that there was something greater than us out there, and because it seemed appropriate, I called that greater power God. Of course, no one knows for sure who or what that source is, so we use faith and what we are taught as our methods of understanding.

Many different religions in the world refer to that Higher Source by different names. I believe no matter what religion you believe in, most people will agree on one point: there is a greater force at work in our lives, a spiritual force beyond our ability to comprehend. Many people pray to that source. I also believe that everyone has the right to choose whom or what they worship and how they worship. What's unfortunate is that religion has been used throughout history to justify starting wars, killing people, passing judgment, and promoting hate and superiority as well as a number of other ideas that were never a part of any scripture or doctrine initiated by any Higher Source. But that's another story.

When I was a child, my prayers were pretty simple:

I prayed for someone to save me from being abused. When I was a young woman, I prayed only when I wanted something, and I prayed with no real faith that I would ever receive it. I would bargain with God and then, when my prayers went unanswered, just shrug it off because I figured praying was futile anyway. Just as I had when I was a child, I thought God did not save me or give me something simply because I wasn't good enough or worthy of a response from Him. And I knew He was right. I wasn't good. So my prayers were without faith.

After Ed's trial, I filled my life with raising my children. Children are one of the true gifts we receive in life, one of the true tests we have to demonstrate our ability to love. I had my daughter, followed twenty-one months later by a son, and then another son three years after that. They are the joy of my life, and I threw everything I had into giving them the love and attention I never received as a child. I was a stay-at-home mother and followed the rules of parenting as written by T. Berry Brazelton, except that we did not go to church regularly as he advised. I tried to get involved with several churches, but I never felt like I fit in. They were too structured and limited for me, and I didn't want my children to be taught under restrictions. So I read books and sang to them. Some of the books were children's Bible stories, and others were about spiritual awareness. I wanted my children to know something about Christianity and also to have a more open spiritual and metaphysical view of important life issues. I wanted them to know that God was there for everyone and that He would be there to help them when they needed Him.

But I still didn't believe He was there to help me. I still lacked faith. What I tried to comprehend for years was the thorny and perennial question: If God gave everyone free will, why was He so selective? What kind of God would say, "Okay, listen up. Everyone has free will, but if you screw up you're going to hell"? I thought, if God were so temperamental and was just waiting for us to make mistakes so that he could punish us, heaven must be a very lonely place.

When I started praying as an adult, I began to ask questions: Why am I here? Why was I abused? Why is life like it is? What is my purpose here? The list of my questions was endless, and I was sure I wasn't the only one asking them. With Ed in jail and my past behind me, I didn't feel like I needed God that much, so I talked to Him only occasionally, and even then I felt guilty for bothering Him with the trivialities of my personal problems. There were people out there with much bigger problems than mine.

After I decided to testify against Ed, my husband, Tom, and I didn't speak of my past until years later. There were many days when I never thought about it. We lived in Atlanta until January of 1991, when Tom was transferred to Barcelona, Spain. This was the turning point for me. Because I had worked in the travel industry, I had developed a passion for travel, and the prospect of living in a foreign country was both exciting and a little scary.

Tom relocated to Spain seven months before the children and I did, which made for a very hard time for me. After my first child was born I had left the travel industry and started my own catering and cake business so that I could stay home with my kids. I was running a business while trying to take care of three young children (they were six, four, and nearly two), plus keep the house orderly and clean so that we could sell it. Although Tom came home every two weeks for a weekend, I received very little support from him. By the time we moved, I was exhausted but ready to start a new life.

This was when my relationship with Tom hit a curve. I had the feeling of being unwanted in Barcelona. He had established a routine in the seven months he had been there, and I wasn't a part of it. I didn't speak Spanish at the time, I had no credit card in my own name, no checkbook, and—more important—no friends. I was more dependent on him than ever. He didn't like this dependence, nor did I, and I didn't like the way I was being treated, as if I were a problem or interference in his life. Things deteriorated quickly. We couldn't seem to get back to where we were before he left. Less than a year later, I packed up the kids and headed back to Atlanta.

I got a job, rented a house, put the two older children in school, and found a babysitter for my youngest child. I was miserable and consumed with guilt at taking the kids away from their father. Tom called me almost every day, begging me to come back and promising me it would be better. I hesitated, but after four months of being a single mother I began to doubt my decision to return to Atlanta. Even though I lacked faith, I started praying to God to help me. I was at a low point in my life and felt lost again. I begged God to tell me what I should do or at least give me a sign.

Then one night, after I had been sobbing and praying for hours, a great calm came over me. It was as if I were being cradled by an angel. I heard a whispering voice telling me to go back to Tom. Suddenly I had clarity. I truly felt like God had for once answered me. The next morning I called Tom and told him we were coming back. My heart told me it was the right thing to do—for me and for the kids. I knew there were still problems to be resolved between us, but I felt I needed to go back to Tom to resolve them. Shortly after we returned to Spain, we were transferred to Madrid. I felt at peace with my decision, and that's when my world changed forever.

I immediately found friends. Soon after, I was asked to join a Bible study group. Because I had never had any formal training in religion, I felt ignorant on the subject and was afraid I would be looked down on, but my friend Carmen convinced me the group would be very informal, more of a social gathering and learning process than a test in theological knowledge. I hesitated but finally agreed, more out of curiosity and a need for friendship than anything else.

That study group proved to be the start of something wonderful for me. Among many things, I discovered the true power of prayer. It was beginning to work for me. We prayed for each other and things happened. We prayed for others, too, and I saw the results, and if things didn't happen exactly the way I wanted, I was still at peace. I found this fascinating. I realized that I'd spent most of my life engaging in *wishful thinking* that I called prayer. It was prayer without faith. Faith is believing and trusting that what you can't see does exist. It's the heart guiding you back to who you are, and if you let it, it's the spirit showing you the source from which you came.

I knew the term *blind faith,* but I thought it was just a metaphor. Blind faith means following your heart, your intuition, and letting it guide you. It means putting the ego aside and taking that leap into the unknown. Faith is a building process. Prayer helped me build my faith: the more I prayed, the more faith I had. It's a give-and-take process. If you ask for more faith, you will receive it. I learned to let myself be guided through the woods of uncertainty to the garden of knowing.

Of course, not every prayer will be answered the way we want it to be answered, and there will be times when we won't like the answer we receive. Tom and I began having problems again after I began the Bible study class. I wasn't sure why. Because of his agnostic beliefs, I never talked about the class to him. But when he asked about my day and I told him that I had gone to my Bible study class, he would ridicule me and ask me, "Are you turning into a 'Bible thumper'?" Even though his sarcasm hurt me, I tried to explain my reasons for going. I understood his feelings were a result of his strict religious upbringing, which had turned him off religion altogether and caused him to question the concept of God. I think he was afraid I would turn into an evangelical like many of his family members, who were constantly trying to sway his beliefs. So because I felt our relationship was deteriorating, I began to pray for him and for us. I prayed that things would get better. But like a parent who tells her child no, the Higher Source will not always give us what we want when we want it. He wants to serve our better good. We must have faith in this. I believe the Higher Source will always give us what we want according to what our soul's purpose is. This is what brings us the most growth. It is also why it is so important to listen to our intuition, to our heart, to our first thought about something.

Your first thought about something is usually your intuition talking to you. This is what connects you to the soul and tells you what's right for you in whatever situation you are in. You have to listen carefully, though, because the ego is swift and sometimes gets in the way.

One day in Bible study we were sharing personal spiritual experiences that we considered to be miracles. I talked about an incident that had happened when I was nine years old, something I now consider my second encounter with God, though at the time it was only an intense feeling I had that something miraculous had just happened. It was also a time when I had not listened to my intuition. I had gone over to a friend's house after school. Her name was Carolyn, and she lived nearby on a busy farm road. After we'd fed her horses, Carolyn decided she wanted to go over to the park across the street.

We were holding hands, getting ready to cross the road, when I saw a car coming. It looked like it was traveling at a high speed. "Come on, we can make it," Carolyn urged, but I was scared because the car was approaching too fast and my inner voice was warning me not to run into the street. Nevertheless, I let Carolyn guide me. She squeezed my hand and bolted, pulling me with her. Suddenly she let go. I fell down in the middle of the road. Then I heard tires screeching. I closed my eyes and grabbed my head, waiting for the impact.

It never came. I heard a scream. I heard a screen door slap shut somewhere in the distance. I opened my eyes. All I could see was a shiny chrome bumper above my head. I was lying under the car, shaking uncontrollably, paralyzed with shock. Then I heard a man's shaky voice. He was inspecting me and muttering incoherent words. Another voice began yelling and asking what had happened. This was the neighbor from across the street, who had run out when he heard the tires screeching.

"Is she okay?"

"I don't know." The neighbor squatted down next to the driver, and they both looked at me. "Are you okay, honey? Can you move?"

I nodded shakily, and then the neighbor gently pulled me out and picked me up into his arms. "I don't think she's hurt," he told the driver, "but she's shaking like a leaf. What the hell happened?"

"I don't know," the driver said. He was crying and shaking his head. "Two girls. I saw them, but I was going too fast. One minute I was looking at my speedometer, wondering how I was going to stop the car. The next thing I knew, the car stopped." He looked at me, then at the neighbor. "Man, I must have been doing fifty, but my foot never touched the brake . . . it's a miracle . . . I swear my foot never touched the brake. I don't know how the car stopped."

I was frightened, but when the man who was holding me said he was going to call my mother, I begged him not to. I knew Ed would punish me for being stupid and clumsy and I would never be allowed to go to my friend's house again. That was all I could think about. I prayed they wouldn't find out what had happened, but as I walked home I had such a strange feeling about the incident. It was like it had happened to someone else and I had watched it from afar.

It never occurred to me that that stopped car was a miracle. I had nearly been run over, but an angel had stepped in to protect me. It took me years to figure this out.

If I had been wise enough to follow my intuition, or first thought, that was clearly telling me not to cross the street that day, I would have known that Carolyn and I could never beat that car. Years later I understood what had happened. I had not listened to my inner voice, and not listening had nearly killed me. The more profound lesson, however, was the realization that we are all being carefully watched over. We all have our angels talking to us, guiding us, and protecting us. God had answered my prayer that day, and neither my mother nor Ed ever found out what happened. This was just another pebble added to my small pile of faith. I told the women in our group that I believed to this day that an angel had stepped on the brakes. The reason why this happened, I can only imagine. Maybe both the driver and I had lessons yet to learn, accomplishments still to make, prayers yet to be answered.

My marriage to Tom continued to deteriorate. I stopped going to the Bible study class, and instead a group of us began reading *A Course in Miracles* and got together weekly to discuss it and other spiritual books. During this time I felt my intuition was telling me that things would not get better between Tom and me. It seemed that the more open and accepting I became of his beliefs, or lack thereof, the less accepting he became of mine. He didn't understand that the books I was reading were a way for me to help myself and were not a threat to him. The more he saw me reading, the more threatened he became and the more his feeling threatened affected our relationship. My prayers changed from, "Please, God, help us get better," to "Please, God, guide me to make the right decision for myself and my children." With this shift, things became clearer to me. I began to understand that while we can't change others, we can change ourselves. Deepak Chopra says, "When we experience the power of the Self, there is an absence of fear, there is no compulsion to control, and no struggle for approval or external power."

But Tom looked at my happiness and independence with fear and suspicion. I believe that on some level he felt I was leaving him behind or that we no longer had anything in common besides our children. Even though the prospect of a divorce after sixteen years of marriage was very frightening to me, I had faith that everything would be okay even if we did get a divorce.

It's all right if a person doesn't have faith in a Higher Source. Sometimes all that is necessary is to have faith in yourself. Believe that you are good and worthy of goods

---

[2]Deepak Chopra, *The Seven Spiritual Laws of Success* (Novato, CA: New World Library, 1994), 11.

things happening in your life. Believe that you have a right to be happy. Have faith in that one thing, and your life will shift.

While I was living in Spain I noticed many shifts. I stopped going to the Bible study class, because I began to feel it was too limiting. I didn't agree with many of the teachings and how others interpreted them. So I turned to books with a more metaphysical and spiritual view, which made more sense to me. Nevertheless, as time went on, Tom became more critical, more threatened by the spiritual path I was on. What seemed so ironic was that I thought it would have the opposite effect and bring us closer. I was finally beginning to feel at peace about my past and life in general, and I thought it could only have a positive impact on my relationship with Tom.

One day I tried to sit down with him and reassure him that he shouldn't feel threatened by what I was reading. I tried to bring up my past and let him know that I was only trying to move forward by letting go of the hurt from my childhood so that I could be a better person. I told him that the books I was reading, books by Marianne Williamson, Neale Donald Walsch, and others, were helping me achieve this. I finally told him that I been sexually abused by Ed, though I still didn't go into any detail. I left it open for him to ask questions if he wanted to. But he didn't. He still didn't want to know.

This lack of interest didn't make me angry, only a little sad because what happened to me was a part of what made me who I am. Even though it wasn't necessary for me to tell Tom everything to be okay with myself, I thought it would help him understand me on a different level. I believe that when you love someone, you want to share *all* your parts, even the ones that you may have once judged to be bad. However, I had enough confidence at that point not to feel afraid of his rejection or be afraid of being judged. I simply wanted him to understand who I was and that I was just trying to heal my mind, body, and soul. I no longer needed anyone's approval. My approval of myself was all that mattered. Prayer is what helped me achieve this new way of thinking about myself. It played a significant role in helping me learn how to love and be at peace with myself.

CHAPTER 17

Learning to Love Ourselves

Healing will come when you confront your pain, forgive yourself and your abuser, and—if you believe in a Higher Source—pray for the guidance and strength you will need to do these things. In order to heal, you have to have faith that you can achieve these things.

So let's talk about love.

It's through love that we can heal ourselves. Learning how to love ourselves will free us from our fear of being unworthy and enable us to see our past experiences in a new light.

Can you look at yourself and say, with absolute certainty, *I love you*? Can you forgive yourself for inflicting pain on your own psyche? It is very difficult to love yourself when you believe you're not worthy. Maybe you're overweight, you're poor, or you think you are a bad person—you're not worthy of love. Even people who have never been abused find reasons to dislike themselves or judge themselves unworthy of love.

When you feel like you don't deserve to receive love, how can you *give* love? If you can't look at yourself and love who you are, how can you expect anyone else to love who you are? If you believe you are unworthy, the energy of that belief is felt by others and the result is that they will eventually think the same about you as you do. If you look to someone else to show you your worth, you're putting a lot of pressure on that individual. But when you love yourself, you stop looking for someone to prove to you that you are worthy of love. You begin to understand your worth and begin to search for someone who values you, someone who appreciates and loves you for who you are and loves you exactly the way you are.

When you love yourself, you stop searching for someone to ease your pain and begin looking for someone who understands it and is willing to love you anyway, not because of the pain but because of who you are as a result of that pain.

If we have learned our lessons well, we will come to understand that the painful seeds of our childhood were planted to help us grow up. We will see who we are in relation to that experience and accept the bits that have made us better and let go of the ones that don't. The pain can go, but often memories must remain for future use. Understanding this fundamental lesson makes it easier to love ourselves. We think that if we can *forget* pains of the past, then our lives will be better. But imagine the difficulty in achieving this forgetting. It's nearly impossible. It's like trying to stop yourself from blinking. You can make yourself stop blinking for a little while, but eventually your eyes will blink. It's essential for their health. Keeping memories is essential for your growing process. But hanging on to the pain of that experience is not essential.

Hanging on to pain takes us away from ourselves. It's often much easier to stay attached to it than to let it go. We stay attached to our pain, for example, so that we won't have to think about who the pain has made us become. We think about the person who inflicted the pain and blame him or her for who we are. We may stay attached to pain because we are waiting for someone else to take it away for us. Sometimes we keep ourselves so busy the pain just can't surface. Sometimes we're so busy looking outside ourselves for someone to take the pain away we lose our connection with the Higher Source. This source can give us the energy that is needed to see our true self or help us understand who we are internally. Hanging on to pain keeps our internal selves covered up.

We have to listen to that internal voice when it talks to us. For example, it may be saying, "You really need to talk about the abuse to someone so that you can move forward." Talking about it to someone you trust releases the pain on that external level, which in turn helps you to begin to release it internally. When we are able to completely let go of pain by whichever methods we choose, we can then get on with the process of loving ourselves.

When we constantly remind ourselves of the pain, we only hurt ourselves more. We feel sorry for ourselves, but that doesn't benefit us. It is difficult to see this because this behavior has become so natural to us that we don't recognize it as hurting ourselves.

Hiding our pain can have serious effects, too. If someone has hurt us deeply and we aren't sure how to deal with the pain, we hide it by reacting outwardly through anger, hate, or possibly some form of addiction, which can really hurt us. Overeating, drinking alcohol, drug abuse, and addiction to sex are some of the ways we try to hide our pain or control it. Someone who overeats because she was sexually abused as a child may be doing it because, subconsciously, she wants to make herself unattractive to future abusers and protect herself from feeling vulnerable. She wants to be in control because she didn't have any control as a child. But the reality is that she is only controlling the external forces surrounding her. She's using food to try to control her life. It will make her feel better. The ego convinces her this is the best way to deal with her pain. But this negative reaction to pain has the opposite effect. Instead of loving herself, she will end up hating herself for her weakness and/or for being overweight.

If we let any type of negative behavior take over, we will never learn how to love ourselves. These negative behaviors will consume us. If we let go of pain and learn how to love ourselves, we become strong with the knowledge that we don't need to control the external forces around us to feel loved or secure.

We might think that loving ourselves is a selfish act. It's easy to convince ourselves that it is. The ego sees loving the self as being self-serving, arrogant, or self-indulgent. But we need to change such a thought pattern.

When the abuse started in my life, I was only six years old. I didn't know anything about hate, but I quickly learned. The first person I hated was myself, although Ed ran a close second. I hated myself and was ashamed for not doing something about my situation. I knew that I wasn't physically capable of moving away from home, but I still blamed myself and convinced myself that it was my fault that I was being abused. Even though I was only a little girl, I had those thoughts. My self-hatred displayed itself externally in subtle and not-so-subtle ways. During the years when the abuse was happening, I would sit for hours, biting and picking at my lips until they were bleeding and swollen. I know it sounds awful, and it was. But this was my way of making myself unattractive to Ed (not that it mattered to him), and at the same time picking at my lips allowed me to inflict pain on myself because I hated myself. It was also a means of control. No one could stop me. My mother used to ask me why I did that to myself, but I could never answer her. As a child I didn't really understand why I was doing it. Ed understood, of course, but he wasn't going to say anything.

As I look back at myself now, I see picking my lips as a habit, a form of addiction like alcohol or drugs. It was an escape from reality that, illogically, eased my pain. I was controlling the external forces around me because I didn't know how to reach my internal force and on some level didn't want to face my reality. I was too young. God was lost to me, there didn't appear to be any angels watching over me, and there didn't appear to be any human being willing to help me. These beliefs validated my feelings of unworthiness.

I carried all these negative beliefs forward and used them to fuel my own self-loathing when things went wrong in my life. It took me nearly thirty years to see the importance of finding a way to love myself.

Once we learn to love ourselves, addictions and controlling our pain through external means will disappear and life will become easier. Loving ourselves frees us to explore our world in new ways. It allows us to open up and let go of these addictions. We don't need addictions anymore.

It's natural to want someone to love us or to want someone to love, but if we first learn to love ourself, our reasons for wanting love change. We stop looking for someone to complete us and instead look for someone to share our completeness with us. We look for someone who will understand who we are and love us because of it. We look for someone who wants to share his or her completeness with us, someone who isn't afraid to reveal him- or herself completely. When you experience a relationship at this level, you will experience significant growth. This is the path to true love. and you will find it very quickly once you change your beliefs about yourself.

The path of self-love is the path we need to put our children on. Teaching them to love themselves is the greatest gift we can give them. We also have to protect them because an abused child will only learn betrayal, fear, and how to hate himself and others. His life will become a reflection of his teachings.

While I was still living in Spain, I saw a father hit his child in a grocery store. I was ordering fish from the fish counter when I heard a child whining and squirming in the grocery cart. He was about eighteen months old, and the father was nearby, looking in the meat bin for something. The child had reached out for a package of meat, got his little fingers around one, and tried to pick it up. The father stomped back over to the cart and screamed at the child that he was bad. He jerked the package out of the child's hand and slapped the little boy across the face with enough force that I could almost feel it. The child screamed out in pain and began sobbing uncontrollably. That's when, with rage in my heart, I walked over to the father.

"Why would you hit your baby like that?" I asked him. "Does it make you feel powerful? And now you want him to stop crying, when you clearly hurt him. How in God's name could you do that? You ought to be ashamed of yourself."

The whole time I was reprimanding the man, he stared at me in shock, clearly unable to believe someone would speak out. The child was still whimpering, and I gently touched his little cheek.

"Love your child like he loves you," I told the father. "Don't hurt him."

That's when the man found his voice. "Mind your own business!" he shouted.

"You made it my business when you chose to hit your son in front of me," I told him. I further told him that I was going to report him.

After I walked away, I turned around to look at them one more time. I saw the father pull the child out of the cart and hug him. He buried his head in the child's tiny shoulder. I heard him say, "I'm sorry, I'm so sorry. Daddy loves you."

I wasn't sure how to go about reporting child abuse to the Spanish authorities, so when I saw the man hugging his child, I decided to drop it. Instead, I prayed that God would watch over them both and hoped that maybe my intervention would help the man see the darkness of his actions. I prayed that he would find a way to deal with whatever pain and anger he was harboring in his own life and fix it so that he wouldn't be tempted to behave that way toward his child again.

Many times it's the strain of everyday problems that cause parents to lash out at their children. Maybe it's as simple as *we had a rotten day* or as difficult as *we had a painful childhood.* But we can't make excuses for our bad behavior. It's important for every parent to understand this so that when a child acts up, we put things in proper perspective and not take out our frustrations on a little kid. It's important not to allow ourselves to react on that external level. That Spanish man who hit his child must have been harboring pain and difficulty in his life, but instead of going within and figuring out ways to help himself, he chose to take out his frustrations on his defenseless son. As a result, he was teaching the boy that hitting and yelling is the way you deal with your problems. Thus the child also learns that he can't trust, he's not loved, and he's a bad person. This is a perfect example of how negative external behavior can carry you away from yourself and how it will have lasting effects on your child.

CHAPTER 18

Moving from Self-Loathing to Loving

Self-loathing becomes an internal addiction. Drug and alcohol use, overeating, anorexia and bulimia, obsessive-compulsive behavior, abusiveness, and violence become external addictions, and that's only naming a few. Any of these addictions or behaviors will prevent you from looking within. They will carry you away from who you really are.

I've fought my own internal battles and addictions. Throughout my teens and early twenties it was drugs, alcohol, and bingeing. It wasn't until after my children were born that I began seeking out ways to discover who I truly am. For a while, I allowed Tom to carry me away from myself. I adapted and lived my life based on his beliefs and desires. I felt like I was being controlled or defined by what Tom wanted. I often put myself last after him and the children. In doing this, however, I wasn't serving myself, nor did I have a sense of who I was. This was making me very unhappy. While we were living in Spain, I enrolled in tennis and art classes and began an exercise regime that really energized me. I also started writing. I could do all of those things while the children were at school, and those activities, combined with reading self-help books, helped me to feel happier about myself. I began to have a sense of purpose. And because I was happier, my kids were happier, too.

Tom did not, however, like my transformation. He discouraged me from writing. He continued to resent my freedom. He told me to find a job. But Spanish law prohibited me from working because I had no residency papers or work visa. My not working became an additional source of contention between us. He put very little value in the fact that I was home every day when the kids came home from school and in the fact that I went to their school three times a week to read and on occasion, cook in their classes, nor did it seem to matter to him that I took care of our home and had a nice meal on the table every night. He thought that, if I really wanted to, I could continue my catering and cake decorating business, though he knew because of cultural differences and the difficulty in obtaining supplies, it would be a very daunting task. It wasn't something I really wanted to do at that time. If I had kept that business, I would have been doing it for Tom and not myself.

I also knew that there was a good chance Tom's company would be moving us back to Atlanta, and it would take longer than the remaining time we had in Spain to establish a business. We had already been in Spain longer than expected, almost seven years, and I knew regardless of whether or not the company asked us to move back to the States, I wanted to return to Atlanta the following year because my daughter would be starting high school and I wanted her to begin her freshman year in a school that she would stay in for all four years. I remembered how difficult it had been for me attending two different middle schools and then moving to a different high school district. It had been hard to make friends, and I had always felt like an outsider. I didn't want any of my children to have that experience. I knew life was going to throw them their own curve balls, but I didn't want to be one of the pitchers.

Our final year in Spain marked eight years of living abroad. More significantly, it marked the beginning of the end of my sixteen-year marriage with Tom. The time spent in Spain had been a blessing because it had given me the time needed to see my worth. I had finally grown to love myself and see myself as worthy of being happy. But Tom didn't like the new me, or should I say, *the real me*. I wasn't angry with him, only sad that the result was we could no longer be together. We began divorce proceedings the year after we returned to Atlanta. It was final on September 10, the day before two jets slammed into the Twin Towers in New York.

The time leading up to my divorce was very difficult. I questioned myself constantly. Was I being selfish? How would this affect my children? What if I damaged them? How could I support myself and my children after not working for more than eight years? What if I failed? I prayed a lot during that time. Tom thought it was his agnostic beliefs that were causing me to separate from him, but the actual causes were his inability to accept me for who I was and his constant need to control and change me. Some people close to him didn't understand either and held the belief that my actions would condemn me to hell. But I was no longer allowing the negative words and thoughts of others to influence me or my decisions.

Being true to yourself and allowing yourself to be who you truly are is the fastest way to growth. It took me a long time to discover this truth. It doesn't have to take you that long.

What is truly amazing is how once you begin the journey to personal discovery, you don't want to stop. Your mind may carry you away from the path sometimes, but if you want it badly enough, your heart will lead you back. Our souls speak through our hearts like little people inside of us cheering us on. Our soul's purpose is to make every experience a blessing. Our soul is the child in us waiting for that special holiday, only we are our own present. Our success in achieving personal growth and self-love is what the soul has been waiting an eternity to see.

Praying is one way to help yourself move closer to self-love and away from self-loathing. Ask for guidance. *Please, lead me back to who I am. Help me to love myself so that I can love others. Help me to see the beauty of this life you have given me. Help me to move away from my pain and into your arms so that I may feel comforted by your warmth and once again know your unconditional love.*

Going through my divorce was painful. My fears and uncertainties often threatened to overwhelm me, but I prayed every day. I asked for signs that I was doing the right thing. What's amazing is that once you're open to receiving those signs you see how quickly they come. For instance, before we moved back to Atlanta, I made a trip on my own to look for a house in the school district I wanted. Because the area I was looking in had the best schools, it was difficult to find a house that would be within my budget. While I knew that with the impending divorce I had to find something I could afford on my own, I also saw that this was a very wealthy area and most of the homes the real estate agent showed me were too expensive. After she showed me twenty homes in three days, my hope wavered. But I clung to my faith and kept my heart open. At the end of the third day and in the last house we had time for, I found my new home. It was perfect. It was exactly what I wanted, and the price was within my range. The validation came when I discovered that the seller of the house was a dear friend of my best friend in Atlanta. Since I don't believe in coincidences, I knew that finding this house was meant to be. I had just been given the sign I had asked for. I was in awe of the powers at work in my life, truly thankful for the gifts and the peace they brought me.

Once you begin the process of asking from the heart, *you will receive.* I have often imagined God saying, "What took you so long, my child?" I believe He's been waiting an eternity for us to understand that He loves us—no matter what. He's only been waiting for our free will to kick in and ask Him for the help we need to move forward in our lives. And for us to believe He is listening.

Because Tom was so firmly agnostic, a member of his

family had once said to me that they were counting on me to change him so that he would make it to heaven. I was dumbfounded. To believe that a person who didn't believe in God would go to hell sounded very narrow-minded to me, especially if that person was a decent human being.

"I can't change him," I replied to her, "but I don't believe he will go to hell. What reason would God have for condemning him and not the next person?" I asked. "What God would give us free will to recreate ourselves and then say, 'But I don't like this bit, so you're going to hell'? What God tells us not to pass judgment, but then does so Himself? Is that your God?"

I then told this person that I didn't believe in hell. I told her I believe we create our own hell and we're living it here on earth. After we die we are able to see this and learn from it and carry our knowledge forward in our next life.

She didn't know what to say, but I could see the wheels of judgment turning in her mind. I had no doubt she was trying to figure out a way to save me, too. As we were going through our divorce, she made her views clear. I was now going to hell for divorcing Tom.

However, I was comfortable enough with prayer and my own faith that I would not allow the fears of others to dictate my actions. My understanding of God made it very difficult to believe that He was so selective and that some of us were better than others. I don't think this is what God has in mind. It is a human misconception, an idea that has manifested itself over centuries of teachings and one we have come to take as a given. We believe in a selective God and this affects our own substandard behavior. This belief causes people to place themselves above the rest of humanity and justify that assessment because of what they were taught—Christians are better than Jews, Jews are better than Muslims, Muslims are better than Buddhists . . . the chain of superiority goes on and on. The problem I have with many religions is that they teach fear in order to control and have power over others instead of teaching the power of love and acceptance. For us to be better human beings, I believe it's better to look into our hearts and ask some hard questions. *What is the right thing for me to do? What form of belief best serves me? How can I be a better person based on my beliefs?* We need to ask these questions without fear that the Higher Source at work in our lives is waiting for us to screw up so that He can say, "I told you so."

The truth is that the Higher Source does not discriminate. I believe we are all truly loved unconditionally, no matter how we behave, because the Higher Source knows our souls, which come from Him and are pure love. He knows we've forgotten this about ourselves, so we make mistakes. In the process of trying to recreate ourselves we have lost sight of Him and we think we can do everything alone and without help. He knows this about us and forgives us, and He never, ever gives up on us.

Once we realize that the Higher Source loves us all equally, then we will move forward and our soul purpose will be revealed to us. We will see and feel the beauty of unconditional love deep within our hearts. We will look at each living organism with new eyes. We will begin to understand that we all came from the same source and stop judging. We will stop being afraid of taking those steps toward growth because we think we will fail. We will begin to behave differently and move through our life with more love and purpose.

You will find joy by experiencing love even in its simplest form. *But you must start with yourself.* All our lives, we search for the secret of joy, and in that moment when we catch a glimpse, our lives change forever. The next time you see a rainbow, remember this and feel the joy rise in your heart. The rainbow is the Higher Source smiling at us and saying, "Here you are. Here is a gift just for you, because I love you. You know what beauty is, but sometimes you forget. So I give you this arch of color so that you may be reminded again how beautiful I think you are, and so that you may also see how beautiful you are." It's His promise not to drown the world and our opportunity to show our appreciation for the gifts we receive.

If we all knew how beautiful we were, how could we hate ourselves? This is the question, the concept we must strive to understand. We are all beautiful, free, and worthy of receiving and experiencing beauty in our life.

Self-loathing hinders our memories. Let's turn off the pain for just a moment and tune in to our internal selves so that we can know our history and hear our souls teach us new ways to become whole. Trust is a good place to start.

CHAPTER 19

Remembering Forrest Gump

There are three things I believe in today. I try to live my life by them to the best of my ability. I believe in myself, I believe in God, and I believe in love. These are conscious choices I've made, and sometimes I'm amazed I've chosen one, let alone all three.

It wasn't until I moved back from Spain and my divorce was final that I came to truly feel this way about myself. I had to find a job so that I could support myself and my children. But because I had not had a job outside the home in over eight years, I was afraid it would be difficult. I needed an immediate and stable income, one that catering could not provide, at least in the short term.

I decided to go back into the travel industry. However, the industry had changed so much that my prospects appeared slim, which threatened my confidence. But once again things seemed to just fall into place. I gave my résumé to a personnel agency that sent me out on my first interview. The company made me an offer that very day. I couldn't believe it. This validated once again that I was on the right path and making decisions for myself that were for the purpose of my own growth. I've come to believe that when we're on the right path, doors open and everything seems to fall into place for us.

Remember the movie *Forrest Gump*? My three beliefs are the three things Forrest believed about himself, though he started at a much earlier age than I did. But there was a synchronicity to his life. Things always seemed to work out for him, no matter where he was or what he was doing, because he never doubted otherwise. Granted, the movie isn't a true story, but there is truth in the message. It's the story about an emotionally abused and handicapped child who grows up without letting blame, hate, or anger affect his ability to live happily. It's also the story of a mother's love for and faith in her child. She knows without doubt that Forrest is a child of God, and this knowledge strengthens her and encourages her to show him that he is an equal in society no matter how much society rejects and ridicules him. Forrest Gump is loved unconditionally. He believes his mother and grows up knowing there is nothing he cannot achieve. He never looks at himself as being odd, nor does he judge others.

What a different world it would be if we could all live our lives as Forrest Gump does and not take someone else's word that we are ignorant or don't belong. Forrest knows who he is. That's the only opinion he needs. He is compassionate and kind, impeccable with his word even when someone intentionally tries to hurt him. He knows the value of human life and cherishes it. He loves and appreciates nature. He believes in God and does not resent his handicap; it only makes him stronger. He's not intelligent in the way we rate intelligence, but he's smarter than most men because he knows that love is all that matters.

I took a powerful message away from that movie: that we all suffer in some way or another (some more than others), but if we choose to, we can move beyond the pain and enjoy this life. Forrest Gump is beaten and belittled by his peers, but he always manages to find the good. And the light that is shining within him, he beams onto others. Each choice he makes comes from his heart with unwavering faith and leads him to the next choice, which always seemed to be for the purpose of his growth. Things always work out for Forrest Gump.

We can make good choices, too. We can let people manipulate and destroy us with the things they say and do, or we can also move away and show those people we will not allow ourselves to feel the pain they are trying to inflict on us. They can no longer hurt us. We can refuse to believe their words or insults because *we know who we are*. For those of us who were abused, we can do as Forrest Gump did—shrug it off and smile because we know who we are. I know this is difficult, but maybe it would be easier if we remind ourselves that at least we are alive and now is the time to prove our strength to ourselves.

Most abused children grow up feeling insecure about themselves because, unlike Forrest Gump, they've never had the opportunity to discover who they are or ever experienced a parent's unconditional love. They've hidden from themselves and others for so long that now they are lost. They grow up afraid. They fear that if they tell anyone they were abused they will be judged harshly. They worry that someone might ask what kind of person they are. "What if she is psychologically screwed up for life?" "How can any abused person grow up to be normal?" "They must be unstable." "What if he breaks?" "What if she abuses her own children?" Our insecurity is so strong that we believe no will ever want to take a chance on loving us because we are "damaged goods."

I had those very thoughts for years. I kept my secrets locked away in that nice, dark corner of my mind so that no one could hurt me with them. As long as they stayed hidden, I thought, no one would judge me.

I wasn't Forrest Gump. He's a grown-up child living his life without fear. I was a sad adult drowning in anxiety. My fear of being judged kept me from looking honestly and frankly at myself. My personal growth was stunted by my thoughts of what others might think if they knew my history. I wouldn't allow myself to let anyone see the real me, the real emotional me, the injured and abused me who had grown up full of fear. Because my flaws were uglier than anyone else's, or so I thought, they were flaws that no one would understand. I knew I would be judged by my outer flaws and not by my inner beauty. I had convinced myself that once people knew I had been abused, their perception of who I was would change. They would look at me with pity or disgust.

I was right. Many people did look at an unreal me. Many people never saw my real beauty. After a while, I learned not to let what they saw hurt me.

One of the fundamental lessons we must learn is not to judge or be afraid or hurt when others choose to judge us. Judging is a way to feel superior to others, which can make us feel somehow better about ourselves. But the real truth is that usually when we judge someone it's because we see something in them we don't like that reminds us of ourselves or we see something in them we are afraid of becoming. If our egos could speak aloud, they would be fast to argue this point, and most of us would never admit to that truth on a conscious level. But when we judge other people, we are looking at their flaws so that we don't have to look at our own.

What's really fascinating—and ironic—is that even those who have never been abused believe they are flawed in some way. They judge themselves harshly for their perceived flaws. They become self-abusers and go through life trying to fix the things they think are bad about themselves or, worse, what they think others think are flaws. They waste a lot of precious energy doing all this fixing.

Our efforts to be perfect are killing us. We all know the saying, "no one is perfect," yet we all want to be perfect. What if we changed that phrase to *we all are perfect?* Wouldn't that make life easier?

We might ask, *if we were all perfect, why would we be here?* To answer that question is to understand that perfection is not an image. Each of us is uniquely perfect. We're all different, but we're all perfect because perfection comes from within. Our souls are perfect, and we all have an inherent beauty that comes from the oneness of God. That's who we are.

If we understood this fundamental truth, we would be figuring out how to appreciate each other's perfections instead of looking for flaws. We would be seeing the uniqueness of every human being and rejoicing in the fact that although we all came from the same perfect place, we're all uniquely different in beautiful ways. We would be living with the knowledge that we are living, breathing elements of All That Is, namely, Love. We've forgotten this truth about ourselves, but Forrest Gump remembers it.

When we judge others, our judgment has a negative impact and dims both their light and ours. If we can learn to stop judging ourselves, we will have cleared a major hurdle. If we can learn to stop judging others, we will see another major shift in our life.

Now is the time to remember who we are and throw away past judgments of ourselves and others. It's time to move away from trying to be perfect. It's time to realize we are perfect just the way we are, no matter who tries to tell us differently. It's time to teach this to our children. It's time to believe in ourselves as Forrest Gump believes in himself.

In the movie, Forrest begins running one day. He doesn't know why he's running, but I believe he's running for love. He's just lost love, so he's running to find it again. His search takes him across the land of purple mountains and breathtaking sunsets. It takes him past the glassy waters of purity to the sands of clarity, and then one day he just stops running. He's finally realized he was running for nothing. He discovers that the love he's been searching for is in everything alive. Love is who he is. Love is who we all are. We should each make a concerted effort to discover this about ourselves so that we never find ourselves running like Forrest Gump.

I've stopped running from the demons of my past. As Forrest Gump's mother watched him develop into a loving human being, I have watched my children do the same. They are nearly grown now and are the pride of my life. It is my love for them and theirs for me that has helped me come to believe these things about myself. It's amazing what the love of a child can do for the soul. Just seeing them smile brings warmth to my heart.

Even though the divorce was difficult for them, too, my three children adjusted to their new way of life like champions. That had to do in part because Tom and I agreed and promised each other they would always come first, and we've both stuck to that promise and have remained on friendly terms. Our children have thus seen that just because two people can no longer live together, that doesn't mean they can't get along and it doesn't mean the kids will be loved any less. What many children of divorce fear most is finding out it is somehow their fault or that when one parent leaves they will stop being loved by that parent. It shows me that what children need to be the best they can be, is to feel loved, and to feel wanted in this world. This should be the easiest thing in the world for any parent to do, *to love their child unconditionally.* But too often we let our personal problems get in the way of love.

Sometimes it's necessary for us to grow up spiritually before we come to understand the value of unconditional love or the ways in which we can receive and use love that best serves us and those around us.

CHAPTER 20

The Value of Letting Go of the Past

The past cannot be changed. When we stay focused on the injustices of our bad experiences, we relive them every day and keep them attached to us. Even those who were never technically abused may be carrying scars from their childhood. Society has taught us that it's okay to blame our parents for our misfortunes and the mess we find our lives in when we're "adult children." We do this because it keeps us from looking too closely at ourselves. It keeps the focus on someone else. If we delve too deeply into childhood memories (or fantasies) and try to analyze why we feel the way we do, we might not like the answer, which is that we have stayed stubbornly tuned in to our pain so that we have an excuse for behaving badly when something goes wrong in our life. It keeps us in that self-centered "poor me" environment, the place that keeps us from thinking about the trauma our own parents might have experienced as children. It encourages us to keep blaming them for our problems. This keeps us from forgiving. It's easier to feel abandoned by God and/or our parents than to take responsibility for our own well-being.

Wallowing in the past prevents us from seeing that all experiences are for the purpose of promoting our growth and understanding of who we are. But when we learn to forgive, we break through the barriers of blame and self-doubt and understand we have lessons to learn in this life. Some are painful and some are pleasant, but they are essentially useful lessons because they can teach us to be better people.

How do we look at the wounds of our childhood as something essentially good? By looking at them as a whole series of events that have brought us to where we are today. By understanding that the more we hang on to the pain, the more we bind it to us, and the more it will only bring us fresh pain. We need to come to a realization that our past experiences only define us to the extent that they help us to better understand who we are in the present. We've had the experience of abuse, but now we have moved forward into a new realm of knowing. We must forgive those who committed crimes against us by looking at those who committed the crimes as not having been in their right minds. They may have stolen the innocence of our childhood, but we can't allow the pain of that experience to continue to hurt us. Instead, we can take that knowledge forward and teach others lessons that no other child should ever have to learn. We can teach our children how to grow into loving human beings so that they can teach their children and stop the cycle.

Abuse makes us vulnerable to pain. It steals all hope

from our lives. It covers our souls with impurities that blind us. It obliterates our faith. These things make it very difficult to release the past. It's not that we consciously want to hang on to ugly memories, but just that we haven't found the strength to let go of them or look beyond them. The task is too daunting. Our hearts are hard, and until they soften with forgiveness we will not understand our purpose.

I carried my past around like a newborn baby. I nurtured it, I fed it, I cried when it cried, I kept it close to my heart. It was better than letting go of it, because whenever something went wrong in my life I could blame it on my past. I used my past as my bat, too. When I made a mistake, the bat from my past was at the ready. When a relationship failed, I pulled it out to take a swing at myself. When I failed at anything, it would come out again. I used my bat to beat myself and others up because I was unable to trust. I didn't trust when someone made a promise, I didn't trust affection, I didn't trust that I was smart enough or that I wouldn't be hurt again. The past can do that to you—keep hitting you over the head. You don't trust letting go because if you do you'll have nothing to blame your behavior or actions on.

That's a hard truth to swallow.

I had to learn how to trust and follow my heart in every aspect of my life. In relationships, I needed to trust that when a man stops calling, cheats, or breaks it off with me, it's okay. Instead of punishing myself and allowing the insecurities caused by my past to come forth and have a go at me with that same old bat, I needed to replace that old bat with new thoughts. No one can give you beauty, wisdom, and worth, because you already own them. I finally understood that needing a man in my life does not serve me, but wanting to share my beauty, wisdom, and worth with someone is a different story. For those of us who carry that bat around we need to stop hitting ourselves with it and begin believing in ourselves.

In his wonderful book, *Conversations with God*, Neale Donald Walsch writes about a response from God about relationships: "It's very romantic to say that now that a special other has entered your life, you feel complete. Yet the purpose of relationship is not to have another who might complete you, but to have another with whom you can share your completeness." How perfect is that? Understanding and trusting that we already own beauty and worth—*we are complete.*

Once we move from looking for external sources to show us our worth and let go of regrets and live in the present, our lives will be happier. Forgiveness is the only way we can do this. Compassion helps us understand the value of forgiveness. When we think about the people who have wronged us, instead of allowing anger, hatred, or regret to fill our hearts, we should try a little compassion. *But,* you ask, *how can I have compassion for someone who has hurt me?*

Begin by looking at that person as a child who's lost, angry, or frustrated. Picture them hurting like you're hurt-

---

[3]Neale Donald Walsch, *Conversations with God* (New York: Putnam, 1995), page 123.

ing. Chances are that their life, like yours, was full of pain. Allow your heart to open with understanding and the knowledge that they can no longer hurt you. You can replace the negative thoughts by simply saying a prayer and asking for help in forgiving and releasing your past. You can heal your heart and the hearts of others by sending prayers of forgiveness toward yourself and those people. On a soul level, those prayers are heard and transmitted. You'll be amazed how much better you feel once you are able to do this. Pray for peace, pray for faith, pray for compassion, and these gifts will come to you. God is not here to deny us anything. It is we who deny ourselves because we lack faith or think we don't deserve anything.

We tend to value ourselves only by what we do, not by who we are. We think our jobs, how much money we make, who we know, and where we live are the things that make us valuable. We tend to care more about how we are valued by others rather than how we value ourselves. This is a mistake. We will never be satisfied with the things we've acquired, and it's very difficult to maintain what we think other people value about us.

There may come a time when we seem to lose control of our lives. That's what happens when we allow others to dictate our lives based on what they think is good for us. We go through the motions of everyday life, filling up all our time without taking any time out for ourselves. Some of us never find our true calling because we are stuck living our lives based on what our parents or others thought was best for us or because we are stuck in the past.

It's not too late to break out of the box we have allowed

others to put us in or the box we built for ourselves. We can do this by valuing ourselves for who we truly are. We can do this by forgiving those who have committed crimes against us because we understand now they were lost souls. We can do this by having faith that when we achieve this release, our lives will take on new meaning and purpose.

Protecting Our Children and Helping the Abuser

Once we move from living in fear to living in love, we see how positively this change impacts our relationships with our spouses, partners, children, family, and friends. We discover all the different emotions that come with changing our daily actions from being fear-based to being love-based. It moves us to a new level of understanding that our ultimate goal is learning how to embrace these changes in ourselves with success. When we learn this, it helps us to help our children.

Teaching our children how to love without fear or condition—and teaching them how to do it well—should be our ultimate goal. We need to teach them how to express themselves without anger, judgment, or shame. We need to show them respect because they are as deserving of respect as the rest of us. We need to protect them and show them how to protect themselves. We need to do these things with a vigilant yet loving hand. If we can achieve this we can begin to terminate abuse in the world.

It is important to look at our children as individuals

with unique personalities instead of as our possessions, as things with which we can do whatever we choose. A child is a human being who is developing a sense of identity from the moment he or she is born. Everything we teach our children is absorbed into their psyches like sponges. Therefore, teaching or promoting fear by way of our words and actions can have a strong impact, both physically and mentally. There's a big difference between teaching children to be cautious of the real dangers (like traffic or drugs or weapons) and teaching them to live fearful lives because we abuse them.

Statistics show that babies who are abused or ignored will early on lose the ability to form relationships or cope in society. Some suffer irreversible mental damage and are at risk of becoming school dropouts, welfare recipients, or violent criminals. How can we blame them for these outcomes when they were never protected as children? When they never received proper love and affection?

I remember reading a newspaper article several months ago about a thirteen-month-old boy who was beaten to death by his father. The father told officials that the child had fallen, but the pathologist's report said that blows of tremendous force would be needed to make such tears in the abdominal lining. He compared the blows on the baby's body to those that a boxer might receive. That baby died from blunt-force trauma to the abdomen. Six months before his death, his family had been reported to the local Department of Family and Children Services. So why wasn't this child protected? How can we live with the knowledge that this little boy, like so many others, died at the hands of someone so much bigger than him? How can we ever let the image of that child's torment and horror disappear from our minds without doing something about it?

What most often happens in our society, as in the case of the thirteen-month-old boy, is that many times when abuse is reported it is ignored or just slips through the cracks. In most states, child welfare personnel work hard to respond to every reported case, but it's a thankless job. Too many social workers are overworked, underpaid, and emotionally drained by caseloads that are far too large.

Children are falling through the cracks all the time. For instance, in the state of Georgia, where I live, of the 24,000 children for whom substantiated reports of abuse or neglect were filed in 2002, 1,155 were returned to their parent/parents and abused again. A report published by the *Atlanta Journal-Constitution* shows that between 1993 and 1999, 844 children in Georgia died after someone reported their abuse or neglect (see www.gahsc.org/terrell/deaths.html).[4] A majority of them the public never heard about because the government kept the reports secret.[5] This still happens today. Under the 1990 Georgia Child Abuse Reporting legislation, access to records was supposed to change and the state's outdated coroners' system was to be overhauled to track these deaths; also, a

---

[4]Craig Schneider & Jill Young Miller, "A Chance to Change," *Atlanta Journal-Constitution* (Metro News, September 2003), C1.

[5]Jane Hansen, "Georgia's Forgotten Children," *Atlanta Journal-Constitution* (Metro News, December 5, 1999).

computerized tracking system was to be created to help officials keep tabs on abusive parents. But it's now 2006 and none of these measures have taken root.

Another sad fact is that often when a child dies at the hand of an abuser there may be an investigation, but the names of those children often go unreported in the media. In my opinion, this namelessness only further removes society from getting involved. Sometimes names are not given to protect the remaining family members, but they are often the ones responsible for the child's death. Ironic, isn't it? We will go to great lengths to protect the abusers and murderers, but *we don't protect the children.*

Child fatality records can be inaccurate and misleading. Child abuse fatalities and conventional homicides are not separated, nor do the records indicate which cases were already in the child welfare agency's caseload. When a child's death is labeled a homicide instead of being subcategorized as the result of child abuse, this obviously undermines our ability to build accurate records. Protective procedures vary from state to state, but what we need is a nationwide system that carefully monitors each reported case so that social workers and child protective services can do their jobs more effectively and each child is accounted for.

But even after abuse has been substantiated, there are many cases (especially those involving sexual abuse) in which the abuser goes to trial only to receive a minimal sentence or get off completely. According to the National Center for the Prosecution of Child Abuse, up to sixty percent of child sexual abuse reports are not believed. This is due, in part, to the difficulty in proving such cases. The center also notes that only nineteen percent of those convicted of sexual abuse receive sentences of more than one year,[6] although that seems to be changing now.

A study performed by the New York Society for the Prevention of Cruelty to Children concluded that there is a reluctance on the part of most Americans to report suspected abuse. One of the reasons the study cited was that such reluctance follows America's tradition of privacy: people are hesitant to interfere or cross family boundary lines for fear of getting involved in something sordid and ugly. Perhaps it's also about fear of being sued or judged themselves. In either case, it is fear that is preventing people from doing what they know in their hearts is the right thing when it comes to protecting our children.

Child abuse of any sort reflects a dark side of humanity that's just too difficult for most people to comprehend. The only way to move away from this form of denial is to publicize every case so that people can actually see the faces of battered or abused children. Statistics are meaningless to the general public. We need to see real faces. It's not going to be pretty, but it's necessary, just as going under the knife to remove a diseased body part is painful but necessary. Once we know something about abuse, we can begin to take action for our children's sake.

I used to wonder what would have happened to me if

---

[6]Paul A. Winters, "Introduction," *At Issue: Child Sexual Abuse* (San Diego: Greenhaven Press, 1998); www.enotes.com/child-sexual-article/39042, 2004.

someone had protected me and reported Ed to the police. I was sure Ed would deny abusing me, sure that somehow my mother would get in trouble, too, and it would destroy my family. Even though child abuse existed in the sixties (and way before then), it wasn't considered a societal problem. It wasn't culturally defined. Those who were caught were often just given a slap on the hand or denied access to the particular child. If Ed had been caught and his guilt proved, I doubt that he would have received the sentence he got twenty years later when my sisters and I turned him in. It was our action *as adults* that brought Ed to justice. If we had testified against him as children, it would not have had the same affect. In the late eighties, when awareness of child abuse was more prevalent than it had been earlier, we were much more capable of explaining exactly what had happened without fear of what the outcome would be—and society was more willing to listen.

Taking action also means we need to think about prevention. Many hospitals and communities offer support programs for new parents. These programs offer prenatal and postnatal support classes that teach child development, parent-child relationships, and adult relationships. But we have to identify the families at high risk. These families would include poverty-stricken families with low birthweight babies, drug-exposed babies, and babies that are sick in infancy. These infants are at the highest risk of being abused by parents with poor coping skills. Hospital professionals and community workers can be the first to recognize these families and reach out to them and offer support. There are even home visitation programs, which in my opinion offer a more holistic approach. These types of programs, which vary widely, offer services to new parents, from in-home parenting education to monitoring the health of the infant. The most important aspect of these types of programs is that they keep the families connected to the community and to hospitals so that social isolation, a proven risk factor for child abuse, doesn't occur. I believe that if all families received support and advice and had healthy role models, we might have fewer abused children. What we need is broad-based funding to underwrite such programs.

Since abuse is often cyclical, we could prevent future abuse by getting help for children when they are still young; otherwise, they are at risk of growing up to become abusive parents. Even if they grow up to repeat the same cycle, it's still not too late to intervene. Yes, it may be problematic, but it's not impossible. Many will be so wrapped up in their own emotional nightmare they only see darkness and don't want anyone to turn on the lights. How do we prevent abused individuals from abusing? We must teach them how their behavior destroys lives. It will be a challenging process to put them in touch with themselves and help them purge the poison that has been in their system for so long. But through counseling and community-based programs, success can be achieved. Many people don't believe abusers deserve another chance and that any parent or person who purposely harms or kills a child loses the right to parent or look after another child permanently. Others believe in preserving the family unit and reuniting the family, no matter what, by returning children to abusive parents except in extreme cases. So who is right and who is wrong?

While I believe it's imperative to remove children from their abusers, I also believe it is important to try and help abusers understand why they behave the way they do and why their behavior is not acceptable. I will not make excuses for anyone who abuses, but I will say that persons who abuse may not be aware of the deep-seated reasons for their behavior. Abusers are ignorant of themselves. They are lost in their own pain and anger. Until they can see the truth of their destructive behavior and address the issues of their past, they should never be allowed near children. Such people are still children themselves, and probably stubborn ones, who do not understand the meaning of love. They do not believe in a Higher Source. They have let fear and rage blind them. They are allowing their ego to control their actions by lashing out at small, defenseless children. Their spirit is lost to them. Of course, there are others who have no remorse and just get pleasure out of hurting or molesting a child and maybe there's nothing more we can do but put them in jail and keep them there.

The first step we need to take in helping every abuser is to *remove the child*. We must show the abuser that every child is worth protecting. Next, we must try to *get to the bottom of the abuser's fears* or to the root of what makes this person want to hurt children. Finally, *we must bring those issues to the surface so we can help him or her get rid of them*. Of course, psychotherapy will take time and money, and we live in a society where we feel no obligation to help these sick people, nor do we want to spend any of our hard-earned dollars on them, especially when we already spend enough to put them in jail and keep them there. Why spend any more money to rehabilitate them? The answer is, *because our children are worth it.*

Maybe if we had more volunteer organizations and community-based programs for the correction and healing of offenders, we could begin to help them. Such organizations are already being implemented in Texas, Minnesota, and California. They believe that when you sit down with a human being and hear his or her story, the situation is no longer abstract. It becomes a question of what incarceration will do to the abuser. Will he be healed? Will she be worse when she gets out? Counseling can be a peacemaking process that in some cases circles around the victim and the offender, creating a support system that helps both to heal and forgive. In California, there is a facility just for sex offenders in which they spend a minimum of six years in counseling, role playing, and other kinds of rehabilitation. Once the offenders are released, they are fitted with a global positioning device to monitor their whereabouts. There are restrictions as to the distance they are required to maintain from children, some of which may be too extreme. But these are just some of the ways we can help abusers break the cycle and in the process maybe help us forgive them.

Marianne Williamson wrote, "When we are shaking a finger at someone, figuratively or literally, we are *not* more apt to correct their wrongful behavior. Treating someone with compassion and forgiveness is much more likely to elicit a healed response. People are less likely to be defensive and more likely to be open to correction.

Forgiveness forges a new context, one of which someone can more easily change."[7]

Abusers are, in essence, *love sick*. They don't understand what love is. It's been the missing force in their lives. We can teach them that love is the necessary element of forgiveness, and once they learn how to give and receive love properly, they will be able to forgive themselves and we can forgive them, too. In the long run, this helps us protect our children.

In order to forgive, we must look at abusers as human beings who, by way of their own abuse, were knocked off track and fell into the black pit of self-destruction. Then maybe we can help pull them out and let them know they can be forgiven. But in order to get back on track, abusers will first need to fill the pit with the acknowledgment of past mistakes and self-forgiveness. We can show them the power of love and help them use love in their healing process. If we give every abuser an ounce of the love he or she never received as a child, *healing can happen.* Only good can come from such an act. It would be a new path to empowerment, a path away from past and into present, a way out of the hell abusers chose for themselves into a life of enrichment where they can begin making new choices that will serve them better.

Of course there are some individuals, like Ed, who may be beyond help, but that is because they choose not to receive it or they are so mentally ill nothing can bring them

---

[7]Marianne Williamson, *A Return to Love* (New York: HarperCollins, 1996), page 83.

back. With such people, all we can do is pray for them and keep children away from them. It is not our job to force change onto anyone. Our job is to guide them in a different direction so they might see more clearly where they have erred, where they might make a conscious decision to move away from that pattern of behavior and into something that better serves them. That is all we can do. If we fail, our children are the ones who will suffer the consequences.

It's going to take a collective force to make sure we are successful in protecting our children and helping those who abuse. But I have faith that significant change can be achieved, because the world is changing. Nearly every day we hear by way of the "Amber Alert" system about a child who is missing or has been abducted or about a child molester who's been caught or a child murderer convicted of his or her crimes. This shows that awareness plays a key role. We see TV shows that target abusers who find children on the Internet. NBC's *Primetime* has done a series of shows about luring pedophiles out of their computer chat rooms, by using actors pretending to be minors. These men and woman are set up to go to a certain address where they believe the child will be waiting to engage in their sexual fantasies, only to find a reporter and police waiting to capture them.

More and more these events are being publicized. On the other end of the spectrum we are also hearing more about facilities geared toward helping those who commit these crimes. All of these things represent a positive shift into awareness and one that I pray will continue its forward movement.

CHAPTER 22

Making Abuse Our Business

The abuse in my life took place more than thirty years ago. Back then, talking about child abuse was taboo. Today there is more awareness, even though we still have a long way to go. It is up to the teachers, doctors, neighbors, and family members of every child to pay attention. People should look for the outer signs, which are usually easier to detect in cases of physical abuse—bruises, burns, withdrawal, depression, and violent behavior are a few. If there are physical signs of abuse, the children will often cover them up.

In cases of neglect or sexual abuse, the signs may be more subtle. These children may have a difficult time looking you in the eye while you are speaking to them. They may be withdrawn or depressed or have a general look of sadness or being lost.

When we see such clues, we need to put away our fear of invading someone's privacy and raise the question of abuse. We need to talk to the child, if possible, and help her feel at ease when asking about her situation. The U.S. Department of Health and Human Services says the recommended age for talking to a child you suspect is being abused is eight years or older. If the child is younger, you should promptly report your suspicions to child protective services.

I encountered a child with some of these symptoms when Tom and I were living in Atlanta. Our daughter, Megan, who was about five years old, invited a friend to sleep over on her birthday. The friend's name was Chelsea. Chelsea seemed different from most five-year-olds because she was extremely shy and fearful of adults. I had already noticed on the occasions when I was around Chelsea's mother how she was very strict and controlling with Chelsea and how Chelsea seemed to be afraid of her. I was surprised that this mother had actually allowed Chelsea to spend the night with Megan because she had never done so before. That evening before going to bed, Chelsea put on her nightgown, took off her panties, and got into bed. When I asked her what she was doing, she told me her mother always made her take off her panties so she "would be more comfortable," and that sometimes her mother slept in her bed and would "touch her down there" to make sure she didn't have her panties on. This little girl started to say more, but she stopped herself and her cheeks flushed with embarrassment. She looked at me fearfully, almost as if she had said too much.

I felt like a hammer had hit my heart. My instinct told me that Chelsea was being sexually abused. At first I tried to rationalize it, but all the signs seemed so familiar. I wasn't sure what to do. I told Tom about it and asked him what he thought I should do, but he didn't think it was any big deal. Because of my own background and knowing what it was like, however, I knew it was a big deal.

The next day Chelsea's mother came over early to get her. I pulled her aside and gently confronted her. I asked her why Chelsea had to sleep without any underwear. Although the mother's face spoke a thousand words, all she said was that Chelsea's skin was sensitive and her panties chafed her and that's why she slept without them. But when I persisted and asked her if it was true that she slept with her daughter, her discomfort turned to anger. She didn't answer me. All she did was shake her head and mumble something incoherent. Then she grabbed Chelsea's hand and picked up her things and left. In my opinion, there was guilt written all over face. That afternoon I called a hotline for child abuse and told them the story. Was there, I asked them, anything that could be done? They said that what I told them wasn't enough evidence to investigate, but they would keep my complaint on file. Shortly thereafter, Chelsea and her family moved away from the neighborhood, never to be heard from again. I felt that I had failed Chelsea. Maybe if I had tried talking to her more she would have opened up and told me other things. I sensed that she wanted to speak up that night but was afraid. That event happened sixteen years ago and I would like to believe if I called that same hotline today, there would be an investigation.

It's true that not every child will be willing to talk, but we must be persistent and loving in gaining their confidence, just as persistent as the abuser is in instilling fear in the child's psyche. If we can make that child feel safe and convince her that it's not her fault and that the person hurting her may need help in order to stop the abuse, the child may be more responsive.

What a child fears most is getting her parents into trouble. No matter how badly the child is abused, a majority of abused children, even when removed from the home, want to go back. They do not want to be encumbered with the fact that they put a parent in jail or got them into trouble. Other children, especially teens, might be afraid of reprisals from the parent once they are sent back home. I found out about these dynamics firsthand when I volunteered at a shelter for abused kids after I returned from Spain. For younger children especially, turning in a parent is a betrayal that saddles them with anxiety and guilt. It goes against their spirit because children naturally want to forgive. If we lived in a society that felt that way and only wished to help the abuser regain his sense of balance and right the wrongs he had done, it would be easier to bring the abuse out into the open and under control. Abused children might be more willing to talk. Unfortunately, there are many situations where this is impossible, such as when the child is too young to speak. Most of the child fatalities from physical abuse in the United States are among children under the age of four.[8]

It's up to us to pay attention and look for the signs and hopefully save these little ones from a tragic end by removing them from the abusing parent. When the child is too young to speak, it falls to medical personnel and relatives who have an opportunity to examine or are in con-

---

[8]U.S. Dept. of Health and Human Services, Administration for Children and Families, *Child Maltreatment 2003* (chapter 4, page 31; www.acf.hhs.gov/programs/cb/pubs/cm03/chapterfour.htm#child).

tact with the child to intervene. Extended family members and neighbors should also stand up when they see something is wrong.

Under U.S. law, every state must require certain professionals to report any suspected abuse or neglect. These are medical professionals, teachers, and law enforcement officials. In some states it's mandatory for friends, family members, and neighbors to report abuse. However, there are times when a doctor or teacher who suspects a child is being abused may not report it for fear of retaliation. They may also find it difficult to believe that someone they know could inflict abuse, so they let it slide the first time and refuse to believe there may be a next time.

But doctors and other health care professionals who treat children are the first ones who have a chance to intercede. When they see solid evidence of abuse in a child, they should report it immediately. Many do so. If they suspect, but are unsure, they need to investigate further to find out the facts and then contact local agencies and law enforcement officials. I know this takes time, time many doctors and nurses don't have, but there are some who do take the time, and for this I applaud them. It was shown in a 2002 study that eight percent of all child abuse reports were filed by medical personnel and 47 percent of reports were filed by individuals.[9] We all need to report abuse when we see it.

---

[9]U.S. Department of Health and Human Services, Centers for Disease Control and Prevention, "Child Maltreatment Fact Sheet" (2003; www.cdc.gov/ncipc/factsheets/cmfacts.htm).

Recently there was a report on television of a woman who stopped at a convenience store in Alabama and saw a three-year-old girl wandering around the store by herself. The child came up to the woman and asked her if she could go with her. The woman became suspicious when the little girl came up to her and asked if she could go home with her. When the woman asked where her mommy or daddy was, the little girl pointed to a man at the checkout who appeared to be in his sixties. The woman's gut told her there was something not right about the situation. She took it upon herself to take down the man's license plate number and began calling local authorities to report the situation. She gave them the license plate number, but they were slow to take action. After four days of hounding the police and doing her own investigating, she found a photo on a missing child Web site that she thought looked like the little girl. She finally persuaded the police to act. They tracked down the man and the woman he was living with. It was quickly determined that the child had been raped. There was also a seventeen-year-old boy who had been abused. The man and the woman were both arrested and, at this writing, are awaiting trial. This was a true case of following your instinct.

There are also times when a person might have valid concerns about falsely accusing someone. There are indeed cases where the person accused is innocent. When we falsely accuse someone, the effects on both parents and children are extremely damaging. Actions can be misinterpreted. Sometimes accusations are malicious, sometimes just an error in judgment. When a child sits on Grandpa's lap and then tells her teacher Grandpa patted her behind, or when a father videotapes his one-year-old running around naked after a bath, or it is considered "abusive" when a mother nurses her baby in public, then we have a problem. It is a problem of being unfamiliar or resentful because we've never experienced such things or we just think we are a better person and we're simply making an unfair judgment. A mother was arrested in Florida for what she thought was exposing her breast while breast-feeding her baby in a shopping mall, but later she found out it was because the person who called the police thought the child was too old to be breast-fed. In this case, the woman who reported the mother had some kind of puritanical view like, "Who do you think you are? You can't expose yourself in front me. I would never breast-feed an eighteen-month-old child, and therefore you're not allowed to, either."

As long as people feel it is their right to judge others, we will have problems. God gave us our nakedness and He gave women the ability to breast-feed their babies. Man invented clothes and man invented the baby bottle.

Making abuse our business takes effort, but we need to make sure our reasons for intervening are for the sole purpose of protecting the child.

I've no doubt that when God looks down and sees the pain we cause our children it must break His heart. We have created our own monsters, and it is up to us—up to the ones who are willing to step up and fight to protect unshielded children—to battle the monsters. We must intervene. We have to take our blindfolds off and pull out our earplugs so that we can see and hear the child's call for help. We must let those cries soak into our hearts until we, too, feel their torment. Then we can take our children into protective arms. We can soothe their wounds and kiss their tears away. We can embrace them and sing away the darkness. We'll wait to hear the sounds of their even breathing as we rock away the pain, and then we'll lie down beside them, heart to loving heart and protect them forever more.

And God's sadness will turn to joy and He will smile with us.

CHAPTER 23

Finding Our Beauty and Following Our Dreams

Moving ahead on our journey through life with forgiveness in our hearts for those who have trespassed against us is tough to do. Learning how to be compassionate and kind every day of our lives takes dedication. Teaching our children to do the same is a daunting task.

Some might think that achieving all these goals in one lifetime is impossible. We're lucky if we can achieve just one. We all get angry at ourselves and at our children. We all judge. We all fail at some point in our life to do the right thing. That's true and that's okay. It's an attitude of indifference that stops us from succeeding; we fail when we don't believe change is possible.

While it may be true that we may never reach that point where we are able to live with an attitude of oneness with the world, where our hearts are full of love for all creatures and we can always forgive our brother or be a perfect parent, but at least we can say to ourselves, *I will try*. We can make a promise to ourselves that we will do our very best. We can make a promise to our children that we will help them do the same and we will protect them along the way. Because it's a very big goal we're aiming at, we can also ask for assistance. If we make this promise to ourselves, then surely that's enough for God. If we just have the thought, plus a little faith, we will see things change in our life. We shouldn't let fear stop us. If we go about our endeavors with love and openness to the universe, our fear can be overcome and as a result we can help our children. We'll begin to see our inner beauty.

There are many stories and fables about finding our inner beauty. Movies like *The Wizard of Oz* and *Forrest Gump* have a similar message. We are searching for something that was always there and can never be taken away because it's part of us. Our beauty lies within us. We may have to climb mountains and overcome enormous obstacles that seem impossible, but it's having the faith and listening to our hearts that will bring us back to ourselves, back to the hidden beauty that lies within each and every one of us. Our beauty was always there. It just got buried by all the impurities of our past or superficial, mundane complexities of the present, which has made it very difficult to see. Opening our hearts and following our intuition will help us uncover our hidden or stolen beauty.

Children come into this world free of fear, guilt, and anger. With each minute, they are creating themselves. We can be their guides on their journey and give them permission and the means to express themselves any way they choose with love and openness. We can be their guides to finding the beauty that resides within them.

By providing our children with a nurturing environment so that they can reach their full potential, we will see the beauty within them blossom. We will surely make mistakes along the way, but if we are teaching with compassion and love in our hearts they will smile in remembrance of those mistakes, and instead of viewing them with anger and hurt feelings, and they will thank us.

My childhood lessons were tough to bear. I said at the beginning of this book that mine is perhaps a grim tale. But it has a happy ending! I have moved beyond my pain and into forgiveness. I have scoured away the blame and hatred that resulted from being abused. I have mended my heart with love. I know I will never forget what happened to me, and that's okay, because I need those memories to help me help others mend their hearts. I know my destiny. I am embracing it with every part of what I am.

Love is what will heal the world. Although I am only one person, I will endeavor to spread around as much of it as possible to heal others I may encounter along my journey. It is my hope to provide love and understanding to those who abuse and have been abused and help them to heal the pain in their hearts so that they might view the world with new eyes. But my greatest hope is to stop abuse on a worldwide level so that all people might embrace the miracle of life.

I hope to show every little girl and boy I encounter how she or he can regain the beauty that was stolen from them. The truth is, it was never really stolen. No one can take the loving heart that exists within each of us. Beauty is not a thing that can be stolen. It is the essence of who we are. It is not a possession. It is part of the humanity that gives each of us the ability to grow.

If we can remember that we own our beauty, always, and that no one can ever take it from us, then we will have learned the greatest lesson of life. Beauty is the essence of love, and love is what we're made of, love that comes directly from the heart and soul of God.

As parents, we have the capability to create a new world for our children. Children are the new souls of the world, and through our loving instruction they will learn the rewards of giving and receiving love. It is then that God will look at all His children and say, "Now this is what life is all about." He will embrace us with joy in His heart and fill us up with the love we've been missing.

God bless the children of the world.
Keep them safe through our wisdom,
Keep them warm through our strength,
Heal their hearts with our love,
Give them peace through our souls.
God bless the children of the world. Amen.

AMY MADDEN is the mother of three children. She has extensive experience as a travel writer for one of the top travel management companies in the world, producing more than thirty-nine news and features articles a month. Amy is also an accomplished, prize-winning chef and former caterer and is completing a cookbook for college students. She is also working on a book that explores divorce and successful parenting. Amy resides in Atlanta, Georgia.